Michael is an experienced parenting educator, speaker and writer. He's also an experienced parent, which gives him some street cred.

He's the author of seven books for parents, six of which can be found at www.parentingideas.com.au

Michael also runs workshops and seminars on various parenting topics. You can find details of past (available on DVD) and future seminars on his website.

Michael thinks kids should help at home, so he's created a 'Chores and Responsibilities Guide' for kids, which you can get free at www.parentingideas.com.au/parents/introduction

Also by Michael Grose

A Man's Guide to Raising Kids
Working Parents
Great Ideas for (Tired) Parents
Raising Happy Kids
One Step Ahead: Raising 3–12-year-olds
Why First-borns Rule the World and Last-borns Want to Change It
XYZ: The New Rules of Generational Warfare

THRIVING!
RAISING EXCEPTIONAL KIDS WITH CONFIDENCE, CHARACTER AND RESILIENCE

Michael Grose

BANTAM
SYDNEY AUCKLAND TORONTO NEW YORK LONDON

A Bantam book
Published by Random House Australia Pty Ltd
Level 3, 100 Pacific Highway, North Sydney NSW 2060
www.randomhouse.com.au

First published by Bantam in 2010

Addresses for companies within the Random House Group can be found at www.randomhouse.com.au/offices

National Library of Australia
Cataloguing-in-Publication Entry

Grose, Michael, 1955–

Thriving!/Michael Grose.

978 174166 948 0 (pbk).

Includes index.
Bibliography.

Resilience (Personality trait) in children.
Resilience (Personality trait) in adolescence.
Child rearing.

155.41824

Typeset in 12.5/18 pt Adobe Garamond by Midland Typesetters, Australia

Printed in Australia by Griffin Press, an accredited ISO AS/NZS 14001:2004 Environmental Management System printer

Contents

Chapter 2: Build a strong, resilient family

Section 4: Promoting resilience 201

Author's note

One of the difficulties an author faces when writing a parenting book is the use of gender when it comes to pronouns. In this book, for simplicity and ease of reading, mostly I have chosen to use 'he', when giving examples or when referring to a child in the singular. No bias is meant!

For Sue – forever

'There are two lasting bequests we can give our children.
One is roots. The other is wings.'
Hodding Carter, 1907–72

Introduction
Setting the scene

What's with kids today?

Ten-year-old Jack was upset. His best friend had snubbed him because he'd heard on the grapevine that Jack had made some derogatory remarks about him. Jack couldn't remember saying anything nasty about his friend, so he took it to heart.

Their argument played on his mind so much that it started to affect his schoolwork. So Jack confided in his dad, who didn't know how to respond. At this point Jack's dad contacted me.

It was a tough one. On one hand, this well-meaning father wanted to help his son. On the other, this was an issue that his son himself needed to sort out.

Jack is typical of many children of his generation in Western countries such as the UK, the US and Australia, who have difficulty with some of life's smaller hurdles. A knock-back in the playground flummoxes many kids. Rather than working out themselves how to resolve such issues, or moving on to find more friends, many rush to get an adult onside to help them navigate the difficulty. Similarly, a minor disappointment, such as not winning a race at school, can feel catastrophic for some kids – they can sulk for days. And having to wait until they reach a certain age before they get their first mobile phone can lead to super-tantrums or, worse, the silent treatment aimed at any adult who won't indulge them. Past generations would turn in their collective graves if they saw some of the self-indulgent behaviour of our younger generation.

Kids today live with modern pressures that previous genera-tions didn't have to face. They grow up with fewer siblings than past generations, which means parents focus their attention far more sharply on them. Recent census figures show that close to

40 per cent of women in their forties have two children and only 25 per cent have three. While there has been a slight increase in the birth rate of 1.75 children per woman in recent years, the size of families is remarkably small – around 50 per cent of families have two children or fewer.

Parents today leave little to chance. Pregnancies are highly planned events. Modern birth control means that adults can not only choose the size of their family but they can determine the age gap between their children with reasonable accuracy. Parents also have the comparative luxury of determining the optimum time to have children, an option that was not considered forty years ago. For many women, a by-product of delaying childbirth is the higher possibility that they will have only one child. They find that they are unable to have a second child due to the fertility decline that comes with age. Conversely, some women who use IVF treatment end up having more children than they'd planned to, as fertility programs can increase the likelihood of multiple births. This perhaps explains the fact that twins now account for one in sixty-six births, rather than one in ninety a few decades ago.

Parents now think carefully about the size of their families. A recent study found that for most parents having a first and second child is a straightforward decision. However, parents tend to agonise about whether to have a third child. The report established that one of their biggest concerns is the strain a third child might place on their financial resources. For today's generation of parents, having children has become an economic rather than a social decision.

Doubtless, previous generations would be flabbergasted to learn that we are thinking twice about how many children we should have on economic grounds, when we live in comparative affluence. But the bar has been set very high in terms of what we want to provide our children with and the lifestyle we expect. Aspirational generation-X parents want a bedroom for every child, the highest standard of education and access to all the opportunities that our increasingly consumer-driven society offers. Concentrating limited resources on such things is now at the forefront of many parents' minds, rather than raising a large family while being content to settle for less. This is the cause of considerable friction between generation Xers and their own parents, for whom four children was the mean number. Spoiling and over-protection were generally not options for most silent-generation parents, as they learned to stretch limited resources.

This level of planning is unprecedented, but such planning and control don't stop when children are born. Like any other project, many kids are carefully managed, measured and monitored to ensure that their development is maximised. Nothing is left to chance. This micro-management of children, and the highly organised lives that many of them lead, is also anathema to parents of the 1950s and '60s, who raised their children in a more relaxed time. Mothers were also more likely to be at home when their children came home from school, which is a bone of contention for this generation.

Childhood today is serious business – for kids, for parents and for the vast number of commercial ventures cashing in on the early-childhood movement. It is great that we have so many resources available, but we need to be careful that we don't organise the life, spontaneity and fun out of childhood. I can't help but feel sorry for many young children as they are dutifully driven from one organised education session to the next. Their lives are structured, timetabled and organised by adults. Parents these days are loath to leave their kids to entertain themselves or keep themselves occupied. The notion of down time or mucking-around time is unthinkable to some modern parents. 'You should be learning something or doing something constructive,' is the motto of many.

Despite the recent recession, today's kids are being raised in a time of relative prosperity, which means their parents have the resources at their disposal to give them the best possible start in life. The majority of today's younger generation live in homes with multiple TVs and access to computers and a range of consumer goods that were considered luxury items a generation ago. As children, the silent generation would have been grateful to have their stomachs full, but today it is estimated that as many as one in three Aussie kids is overweight or obese. The statistics are mirrored in other Western countries such as the UK and the US. Immunisation programs, improved child-health services and prenatal care have dramatically lowered infant mortality rates. However, we are at risk of replacing one health issue with another.

With greater affluence comes the propensity for adults to instantly provide what children want or pester them for. However, parents need to bear in mind that delaying gratification is not only virtuous but actually good for children in the long run. Studies have consistently shown that educational and social outcomes tend to be better for kids who are able to defer gratification rather than get what they want immediately.

Our consumer culture is both all-embracing and persuasive. There is little that can't be bought these days. Gifts and snacks are bought, rather than made at home. Clothing is rarely mended. Even simple games such as noughts and crosses have commercial versions. Kids also place enormous pressure on their parents to keep up with the Jones's kids. The rule of thumb that many children work by is 'You get what you can bargain for,' and in this way they place inordinate pressure on their parents. Marketers now recognise the effectiveness of pester power, hence the increasing number of advertisements that target children. It is easy for us to forget that there is a difference between a want and a need, and we can have a hard time convincing our kids that even though they may want the latest consumer item, they do not actually need it.

Safety first

Today's young are being raised at a time when social and physical environments appear hostile and parents are plain fearful for their children's safety and well-being. I was in Britain in 2007 when toddler Madeleine McCann disappeared from her parents' holiday home in Spain. The media saturation of that event heightened parental anxiety over child safety everywhere. There is no evidence that the world is a more dangerous place for kids now than before Madeleine went missing, but the massive media coverage of the event and other similar tragedies mean it can feel more dangerous.

It seems that the concept of 'stranger danger' from the 1980s has been joined by one of 'danger from within', which has made parents ever more anxious. Many seem to hover like helicopters wherever their children gather. A survey of seven- to fourteen-year-olds in the United Kingdom found that they fear strangers more than they fear being hurt in a road accident, despite the fact that it is far more likely they will be hurt in a road accident than by a stranger. Although both are real risks that children should be aware of, it can be argued that children and young people today don't perceive risk realistically.

Add to this the highly litigious nature of our community nowadays and we are left with a safety-first mindset, which dominates the thinking of parents, educators and other professionals. Such a mindset contributes to a more sedentary lifestyle and reduces children's ability to assess risk. Outdoor playgrounds are an example. They are now so safe and sanitised that many of them have become boring and without challenge. They come with built-in restrictions. One of the developmental tasks of childhood is the exploration of a child's physical potential, which requires a measure of challenge in their environment. Frequently, challenge is accompanied by a degree of danger. So when we remove elements of danger, we also risk removing the challenge for children.

The removal of risk goes against the notion that many children are heuristic learners, who learn from experience rather than heeding well-intentioned advice. Sometimes that experience is negative and children will be hurt, ending up with scrapes and bruises; maybe even broken bones. But children will learn little about predicting risk and may even become reckless if all the dangers are removed from their environment. The mark of a civil society is the way we treat and care for our most vulnerable members – the elderly and children. While it would be insensitive to be flippant about children being hurt or injured, we need to be careful that we don't do them a disservice by eliminating even the mildest of dangers, inadvertently putting them at *further* risk in the process.

The trouble with the child-focused, safety-first way of bringing up kids is that we're in danger of raising a generation who don't have the intestinal fortitude to handle some of the bouncers that come their way. These are bouncers that past generations would have routinely batted away without blinking. Parental aversion to letting offspring take even safe risks robs many kids of vital opportunities to develop problem-solving skills and coping skills, which are necessary for resilience.

Being a parent is more confusing than ever

'Parenting is the world's hardest job' is one of the great clichés of modern times. Almost every introduction to one of my parenting talks is prefaced with the fact that parenting is the world's hardest job. Raising kids is challenging. It always has been and always will be. Every generation of parents has had their specific challenges. If you raised your kids during the Great Depression, simply feeding them was a challenge. Kids with full bellies were measures of effective parenting. If you were raising your kids after the Second World War, there was a shortage of resources. Infant Welfare Centres had to be built, new schools were constructed and teachers were trained en masse to cater for a burgeoning population of children.

Today's parents have challenges of a different sort. A lack of time to devote to their children has become a big issue: the choice of many new mothers today to stay at home and care for their children full-time can only be seen as a reaction to the image of the frazzled working mother that has grown up in the past decade or so. Modern technology is irrevocably changing the parenting landscape, making it both easier and harder to navigate. Staying in touch with your kids has never been easier, as they are only ever a text message or call away. Yet keeping them safe has never been harder, as communication technology means that even in their bedrooms they are connected to a whole new world, which includes online predators and bullies. Many children and young people have parallel lives – an online and offline life – complete with two different sets of friends and acquaintances. This requires new approaches and throws up questions that parents a generation ago didn't even consider.

In the face of these changes, many parents feel powerless and confused. Others are unsure of their place in the parent–child relationship. 'Should I be my child's friend or his parent?' 'How do I effectively discipline my child and still maintain a strong relationship?' Ultimately, 'How should I raise my children to be able to take their place in the world?' is a big question for many.

Raising kids to thrive

Today's parents, like parents of any generation, want the best for their children. They want the full package: that is, they want their children to be successful, to achieve their potential, to be happy and to enjoy their relationships. Kids live with this pressure. Childhood anxiety is rampant. Its rise is due to a number of factors: the faster pace of life, less down time and their parents. Kids pick up many cues from their parents, so anxious parents beget anxious kids.

Kids who thrive rather than survive

Most of us survive our parents, despite their hang-ups. But some people raise their kids in ways that enable them to thrive under their stewardship. Their parenting is a growth experience, rather than one to recover from.

This book presents a series of ideas and suggestions that will help your kids do just that – thrive under your parenting, rather than merely to survive it. It is a book of practical strategies rather than a book of parenting theory. For those of you who like frameworks and theories to help you make sense of the world, rest assured that the ideas presented all fit under the 'authoritative parenting' framework, which the majority of the current research indicates is the most successful parenting framework. Certainly, it has greatest acceptance among parenting professionals in Western countries today. Authoritative parents search for a balance between warmth and firmness in their child-rearing. Their disciplinary methods are supportive rather than punitive and they aim for self-regulation. Authoritative parents influence rather than control their children and use a range of strategies to build relationships and give their children a voice in the family enterprise.

Allied to making sure kids thrive is the notion of resilience. Resilience is very much a twenty-first century concept. With families shrinking, parental anxiety reaching all-time highs and communities rapidly becoming risk-free, developing resilience in kids is of national importance. It is the number-one child-rearing concept that parents and teachers need to get their collective heads around.

Some kids are resilient by nature – their temperaments help them to be mentally tough. You know those kids. Persistence is their trademark. Whether they are trying to win an argument with a brother or sister, complete their homework or help their team win a game of sport, they won't give in. They get straight back up after a setback or disappointment. Rejection in the playground doesn't faze them. They are flexible enough to cope with changes such as moving from one school to another. They keep working hard in school even if they don't succeed at first. They have resilient spirits.

Unfortunately, not every child has such natural resilience. The good news is that most of the research into the area indicates that resilience can be developed, particularly when parents themselves are resilient and actively foster it in their kids.

Resilient kids share four basic skill sets: independence, problem-solving, optimism and social connection. There are many ways parents can develop these skills, but it is crucial they allow their kids to fully contribute to the family. By developing children's self-help skills, parents promote independence and resourcefulness.

Parents also need to resist sorting out children's social problems and skill them up to solve their own friendship challenges. Sometimes parents can create more problems by interfering in children's disputes; it is better to coach kids through their more challenging moments and review what they may have learned so they can react appropriately next time.

In Jack's case, the rejection by his friend was unpleasant but not abnormal. Kids at this stage can be cruel to each other. Misunderstandings are common. The best way Jack's father could help his son was to listen to him, show him understanding, but also to see this incident as a teachable moment. I advised this dad to lead his son through some possible solutions and to show faith in Jack's ability to solve the problem himself. A genuine show of faith in kids' abilities to cope, rather than a 'get over it' attitude, gives them great hope when they face difficulties. The hardest part of parenting is keeping kids' chins up when life doesn't go their way.

Children learn optimism at home. As I shall explain in more detail in chapter 4, American psychologist Martin Seligman, the author of *The Optimistic Child*, found that kids pick up the explanatory style of the parent they spend most time around, usually their mother, by the age of eight. So a parent's optimistic, can-do attitude pays off.

Regular, positive parent–child interactions are perhaps the best way for kids to pick up basic social skills that enable them to interact with their peers, as well as more subtle resilience skills such as humour, goal-setting and persistence. So parents need to look for as many opportunities to spend time with and talk to their kids as possible.

Children's life experiences contribute to their resilience. The seemingly small disappointments that kids experience, such as not being invited to a party, not being picked in a sports team, or not achieving success in a school project help them to learn to cope with hardships and frustrations. Coping with minor developmental issues such as change, sibling conflict and even failure builds up a psychological hardiness that is invaluable when they face some of life's big challenges in adolescence and beyond.

Parents also need to put children and young people in situations where they must draw on their resourcefulness. Camps and adventure activities are great ways for kids to stretch themselves and test their problem-solving and coping skills. My second daughter believes an eight-day adventure camp she went on as a fourteen-year-old was the defining event of her early adolescence. It involved real physical endeavour, which stretched her to the limits, literally bringing her to tears on many occasions. It was the first time she realised that she could cope with being separated from her friends and family, as well as the comforts of home. One year later she went on a six-month student exchange to the other side of the world. While away she frequently drew on the coping skills she had learned on her eight-day camp to overcome homesickness and deal with the challenges of living in an unfamiliar environment and culture for such a long time.

Promoting resilience in kids is a continuous process. It requires parents, teachers and other adults to look for opportunities for the children they look after to stretch themselves socially, academically and even emotionally. It also requires parents to see some of their children's difficulties and hardships as valuable learning opportunities, rather than catastrophic events that will scar them psychologically. It's worth remembering that the stronger the wind, the stronger the trees, so if we want our kids to be resilient it's best not to be afraid of a little wind. In fact, we should welcome it every now and then.

How should we raise our kids?

Currently, there is some confusion about how best to raise kids in this fast-paced, modern world. The perception that the world is a dangerous place is causing us to closet or over-protect our children. We have a greater propensity than our parents did to satisfy our children's material demands, so we run the risk of raising an indulged generation. Many children currently grow up with an exaggerated sense of entitlement to rights, freedoms and goods, which are often way beyond their means or grasp.

In many ways, today's parents are misguided about the most appropriate way to raise kids. Although families are smaller and parents' earning power is greater than those of previous generations, the lack of time available, rapid changes in communication technology and the commercialisation of childhood make parenting decidedly tricky. And I'm not sure today's parents are as well-prepared as those of past generations to raise children. Certainly, by having kids later in life they are putting more years between their own childhoods and their children's developing years. We live in a world where children under the age of fifteen are less than 20 per cent of the population, so when many first-time parents hold their newborn, it's the closest they've been to a baby for a decade or more. No wonder these new mums and dads cry out, 'Now that I've got this kid, how do I raise him?'

Your job as a modern parent is no different to that of a parent of any era – it's to make yourself redundant from the earliest possible age. Redundancy has always been the aim of parents, and always will be. In the past, when families were larger, parents were intent on developing a sense of independence in their young. There was no other possible way of parenting. If you had five or six kids and none of the labour-saving devices we have today, parenting meant teaching your kids to look after themselves, or to look after each other, so that you could attend to the child that needed you most, usually the youngest. The aim of parents in large families was to teach kids to fend for themselves, as you couldn't possibly attend to all your children's immediate wants.

Large families are more tribal, with natural hierarchies emerging. The eldest child usually has more rights than his or her younger siblings, and greater responsibility. 'You wait your turn' is the message that younger siblings generally learn by osmosis in larger families. At the same time, 'Look after your little brother while I go down to the shops' is the trade-off that occurred between parents and children in the past.

There is no going back. Around 50 per cent of Australian families today have two children or fewer. But parents can still raise their small families with big-family principles. This is the challenge I pose for parents. Raise your small family as if it were a large one – of at least four children – so that redundancy is your aim.

Parenting is a trade-off between giving kids space to grow away and creating opportunities for intimacy. In small families, intimacy is easy. Giving your kids room to grow up without a parent looking over their shoulder is the challenge.

Growing up and growing away can be stifling in families where parents want to be involved in the minutiae of their children's lives. In large families, it's the opposite. Gaining space from parents is relatively easy when there are four or more kids, but the chance to develop one-on-one relationships is lower. There will always be at least one who is left out when there is a gang. But that's the way of large families.

Many readers who grew up in large families will probably be howling me down by now, saying that no one was left out in their family, that everyone was loved equally. Everyone may indeed have been loved equally, but it must have been much harder to divide evenly the scarce parental resources of time and attention: in larger families some children inevitably get more than their fair share. In some families, siblings make up the parental shortfall. In others, kids learn to go without and develop self-sufficiency a lot earlier than others. I suspect this is the reason that middle children usually leave the family first: they don't have the same strong sense of attachment to their parents as eldest or youngest siblings.

The thriving way

Using large-family principles is at the heart of the thriving way of raising kids. It's not a return to the past. Rather, it is a recognition that if we are to prepare our children adequately for the future then we need to take a step back and provide an environment that develops their confidence, their character and their resilience. These three qualities will enhance our children's prospects of future success in all areas of life, including their relationships, their family and their work.

These qualities don't develop in a vacuum. They may develop by accident, but I wouldn't count on it. They best develop in an environment where parents and teachers purposefully adopt principles and techniques that promote them. Nor do these qualities grow independently of each other. The development of each impacts on the others. When kids develop a greater sense of self-confidence, they usually behave better and they are more likely to bounce back from setbacks, particularly social injustices.

Defining characteristics and human qualities is always tricky. We all make our own definitions that are relevant to our lives. Confidence is about taking your rightful place in the world and grabbing your rightful space. It is about making the most of the opportunities presented to you. Confident kids take more learning risks and are likely to challenge themselves more than kids who are low on confidence. They are less likely to place limits on themselves or their achievements.

Character refers to the attitudes and behaviour a child develops to maximise his or her success. We live in a world that's increasingly attracted to personality rather than character. In these days of reality television, MySpace and YouTube, where anyone can have his or her fifteen minutes of fame, personality seems to take precedence over character. But personality is superficial. It's skin-deep. Personality may attract initial attention, but it won't guarantee success. Character more than likely will. Character has greater substance. It has depth to it. Character relates to values-driven behaviour, impulse-control and self-discipline. The development of character in children is at the heart of effective child-rearing.

Resilience, the third characteristic in the thriving trilogy, refers to children's and young people's ability to cope with the setbacks and hurdles that life throws their way. Resilience is a term that's thrown around a great deal these days. It is used to describe the state of the economy, the environment and even sporting teams. In fact, it can be used so much that it begins it lose its potency, particularly in terms of parenting and child-rearing. But when discussing child development, it has enormous significance. Children need to be resilient. They need to be able to bounce back from life's bigger and smaller setbacks. They need to experience the gamut of emotions that come with loss, failure, disappointment and other childhood hardships; they need to face frustrations and difficulties so they learn they can cope when life doesn't go their way. Resilience is linked to good mental-health habits and to a child's success in school and beyond.

The thriving trilogy

Confidence   taking their place in the world
Character   developing the behaviours and attitudes to succeed
Resilience   coping with setbacks and hurdles

Thriving principles

So how do you raise a child with confidence, character and resilience? As I've discussed, some kids are predisposed to have these qualities, but certainly environmental factors, including parenting, play their part in developing them.

Here are ten thriving, big-family parenting principles that, when used consistently and persistently by parents, will promote the development of these characteristics in children and young people:

1. **The self-sufficiency principle.** Develop self-sufficiency in kids from the earliest possible age.

2. **The problem-ownership principle.** He who owns a problem, solves a problem.

3. **The choice principle.** You can choose how you act, think and behave.

4. **The adaptability principle.** It's better to help kids adapt to situations, rather than change situations to suit them.

5. **The teaching principle.** Parenting is a never-ending teaching activity.

6. **The family-first principle.** Focus on the family, not on individual children.

7. **The shared-responsibility principle.** Involve kids fully in the family enterprise.

8. **The cooperation principle.** Cooperation in families is won, not demanded.

9. **The relationship principle.** Relationships give you leverage and need to be nurtured.

10. **The community principle.** Small-town mindsets rule, bro'.

1. The self-sufficiency principle

My mentor in parenting, Maurice Balson, author of *Becoming Better Parents*, first published in 1981, used to drum into his students in his psychology lectures, 'Never regularly do for children the things they can do for themselves.' This message is one that resonated strongly with me, and two decades later it's more pertinent than ever. It's a message of independence that has broad meaning and fits the 'raise your small family as a big family' mindset. It means that when kids are capable of doing a task such as dressing themselves, making their lunch or filling out an income tax form, you skill them up so they can do it themselves. As I mentioned earlier, your basic task as parents is to make yourselves redundant, and that only happens when your children become self-sufficient.

2. The problem-ownership principle

Kids are adept at making their problems their parents' problems. Nothing wrong with that to a point, as a problem shared is a problem halved. But in some cases, they don't simply share the problem, they put it solely on their parents' laps to sort out. The problem-ownership principle applies to many situations, including eating, dressing and relationships. A child who has a relationship breakdown with a sibling needs to do their best to mend fences, rather than run to their parents to sort it out. Similarly, when a parent has difficulty with a child, he or she needs to resolve it with the child, while the other parent plays the role of a neutral bystander. The problem-ownership principle promotes personal responsibility, which is the cornerstone of character and resilience.

3. The choice principle

This is a powerful principle that needs to be embraced by parents and children alike. We can all choose how we respond to situations and events. We are not the victims of circumstances, nor prisoners to the past. Kids can choose to be happy or to be grumpy. They can choose to be grateful for a gift from a relative or to be ungrateful. They can choose whether to stand their ground and argue with a sibling about who should clean up the mess in the living room, or simply clean it up because it's the right thing to do. They can fight with a friend or walk away.

The notion of choice is not something you can teach kids

straightaway. Young children don't understand it. But it can be developed and reinforced by parents over a period of time, when different situations arise. Making good choices is the ultimate in personal responsibility and resilience. Choices can extend to thinking as well as behaviour. The notion of positive framing, which I'll discuss later in this book, is an example of a child choosing how they think about a situation or event.

4. The adaptability principle

Children and young people are frequently placed in situations that are not to their liking. They may have a teacher who they don't get on with; play in a sports team that always loses; or eat food they are not used to on school camp. Children are adept at pestering their parents to rescue them or change a situation to suit them. This is okay when a child's physical or psychological safety is at risk, or long-term harm is likely if no change is made. If not, it's better for kids to cope with these situations themselves. When left to their own devices, children usually develop their own coping mechanisms and adapt their thinking or behaviour to deal with a situation that's not to their liking.

5. The teaching principle

Parenting is all about teaching. It always has been and always will be. Whether it's a mother teaching her kid to be self-sufficient or a father passing on some wisdom or a little lesson through a story, effective parenting is inextricably tied up with teaching. Lack of parental time is the enemy of effective teaching. When life gets busy for kids and parents, teaching skills of independence and coping often stops. It's the 'Velcro' effect. That is, it takes time to teach a young child to tie their shoelaces and for him to practise until he can do tie them himself. Sometimes it's easier to do it yourself, or just buy shoes with Velcro. The Velcro effect can spread to other areas of life. It's expedient, but not effective in promoting a sense of independence in kids.

Thriving parents recognise that life is full of teachable moments. They are on the lookout for these small moments, seeing kids' problems as valuable learning opportunities.

6. The family-first principle

Parents as family leaders need to make the welfare of the family their priority, rather than focusing solely on the individual needs of their children. This means that at different times all children will need to give way to others, or adapt their needs to fit in with others'. The focus of parents of small families frequently shifts to satisfying the needs of individual children. This promotes in kids a sense of entitlement, or a sense of 'me' rather than 'we'. Ironically, the focus on family is always in the best interests of individual kids. Strong families are best placed to raise kids that thrive.

7. The shared-responsibility principle

This is a challenging principle for modern parents, and a powerful one. It means that it's not a parent's job to take responsibility for the running of the family – everyone has a stake in the enterprise. I'm not suggesting that parents don't lead the family. Effective families need strong leadership from parents. But the most effective leaders share around responsibilities. So it's not your job to make sure chores are done, it's everyone's job. If that sounds a little chaotic, then relax – it's not. It's a sensible division of the load, involving delegation, shared decision-making and shared problem-solving, according to each child's development and ability to contribute.

8. The cooperation principle

Cooperation between family members is a tenuous thing. It's based on goodwill and trust, and cannot be demanded or gained through manipulation, bullying or the use of guilt. It is won through the good use of language and is based on the notion of mutual respect. Cooperation is the result of strong relationships and is the embodiment of 'doing what the situation requires'.

9. The relationship principle

Relationships are tricky things in families. They are dynamic and ever-changing. Loving each other and liking each other are different things. Kids may love each other, but they won't necessarily like each other. Same goes for kids and parents. Unconditional love is one thing, but actually liking each other can be a stretch at certain times. The key to effective families is spending time building relationships between each other. You don't have to do too much together, just try to enjoy each other's company.

10. The community principle

Parents struggle when they raise kids in isolation. It takes a bunch of people, including relatives, friends and professionals to raise kids. Forget the notion of 'it takes a village to raise a child'. Give me a small town any day. Better still, give me a regional centre that's big enough to have all the services needed to bring up kids, but small enough for kids to know people and for them to know your kids.

Right now, parents are a little too precious about raising their children, seeing it as a private responsibility. They are likely to challenge other adults if their way of dealing with kids differs from their own, rather than embrace the differences as being part of the healthy development of kids. Parents can get too close to their children and fail, at times, to see the wood for the trees. Professionals, particularly teachers, are useful allies for parents, as they often have greater perspective and broader experience of children's capabilities at different ages and stages.

The triangle of parenting success

Effective parenting is linked to three distinct aspects: family culture, family structures and communication tools and techniques. These three aspects can become your triangle of parenting success if you get them right. Family culture includes your values, atmosphere, and parenting style. Structures include such things as family rituals, the use of routines, the rules and boundaries you put in place, and the rites of passage you use in your family. These structures teach kids about appropriate behaviour and prevent poor behaviour. The third aspect in the triangle refers to the communication techniques and tools you use to promote confidence in kids, gain cooperation and to promote harmonious relationships within your family.

1. Culture

Parents who follow the thriving way make sure their family culture is a positive, pleasant and supportive one. Kids receive more encouragement than criticism. Forgiveness, honesty and tolerance are openly practised and modelled. The prime values that drive parents are shared responsibility, self-sufficiency and mutual respect. The first two have been covered above, while the latter is a challenging one for many parents. There has been a move away from the old notion of respect in recent decades, when kids automatically respected their elders. Respect in relationships is no longer hierarchical, but mutual. We treat each other in respectful ways. That means you treat your kids as you would like to be treated. So smacking and criticising is out. Respectful methods of discipline, such as using logical consequences, are in. The challenge for parents is to expect kids to treat them with respect. That means we don't become slaves to them and we respond to their respectful treatment of us. Sometimes that's hard work.

2. Structures

Effective families are usually orderly and have an identifiable sense of structure. A strong sense of routine is evident, particularly around morning activities, after-school activities, mealtimes and bedtimes. These routines make life predictable for kids, making it easy for them to behave well. Parents make good use of rituals to maximise opportunities for communication and teaching. Mealtimes, birthdays and other celebrations are regular and have a stamp unique to the family. Rules and boundaries are consistent rather than rigid. Kids know what's expected, and understand that parents will use consequences that are fair and reasonable to promote a sense of personal responsibility. Rites of passage are also evident, and are used to grant kids greater rights and freedoms as they get older.

3. Tools and techniques

The third aspect of the triangle of parenting success refers to the tools and communication techniques that we use on a daily basis to teach and train our kids, get cooperation and to promote confidence. Parenting books are full of techniques and tools parents can use. 'How can I speak so my kids will listen?' 'What can I do to encourage my kids to get on with each other?' 'What do I do with a child who is too shy to make eye contact with adults?' These are questions about technique, rather than structures and culture.

To make changes and improvements in family life, it's important to look at all three areas, not just the communication techniques and tools. Check out your family's culture. If you're not sure how to define it, just ask your kids to tell you about the family. Alternatively, imagine what they would say about it. Then stand back and look at the behaviour and values your children share. If they are all independent, even your least independent child, then self-sufficiency is a strong family value. If they are generally happy and good-humoured, your family atmosphere is likely to be friendly and fairly relaxed. Take a look at your structures. Are your routines child-friendly and predictable, or does chaos reign? Do you have known limits and boundaries, or are you wishy-washy about your kids' behaviour, with low expectations? Do you have rituals in place that bring the family together, or are you a laissez-faire family that acts on a whim? Are rites of passage evident, or do you grant kids greater freedom and more rights when they ask for them? Take a look at your structures to make sure they are working for you and your family.

Use the triangle to guide you on your way to raising your kids to thrive. It's a powerful model, with broad application.

Culture
(values, atmosphere, parenting style)

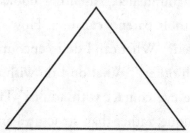

Structures
(rituals, routines, rules,
habits, rites of passage)

Tools and techniques
(language, tools you use
routinely use)

Section 1

Getting the foundations right

Chapter 1

Start by building your own resilience
as a parent

Introduction

Strong families benefit kids. The family is a child's first group, and environment plays an important role in shaping attitudes, thoughts and behaviour. Parents are the most significant part of a child's environment, particularly in the early years before school. Not only are parents children's first teachers, they are kids' prime influencers, impacting on their self-esteem and self-worth.

Most of a child's behaviour is aimed at finding his place in his family, and many of a child's early relationship lessons come from getting on with siblings and parents. Resilient families are best placed to raise kids to thrive. Kids love the stability of strong families. Kids can take risks and know they can fail when they have a strong family to retreat to, which nurtures and accepts them.

Building strong families is seriously hard these days. It takes confident parents, who are willing to assert their authority and their personality on their family so that they stay strong, and stay together.

In this section I will look at how parents can build their own resilience, and at strategies they can use to forge the family bonds that lay the foundation for kids to thrive.

1. Put yourself first, some of the time

Many parents function in a state of near exhaustion. Tiredness and child-rearing go hand in hand for many. It shouldn't be that way. It's one thing if you have babies or toddlers, as they are at demanding and time-consuming stages of development. But when parents stay tired throughout all their children's life stages, it strains family life and can make parenting feel a chore.

It's hard to raise kids to thrive when you are always tired. It's hard to be positive when you are exhausted. It's hard to nurture when you have nothing more to give. Parenting takes a lot of physical and mental energy. Kids by their very nature take more from us than they give. We need to replenish ourselves if we are to be effective, particularly over the long haul. Anxious, pessimistic parents teach their children to be anxious and pessimistic, just as upbeat parents teach their children to be positive. There are no guarantees, but it is easier to be optimistic about life when the parent you spend most time around feels good about his- or herself and life in general.

Modern parents are very busy people. Full-time or part-time paid employment is something that most of today's generation of parents has in common. Kids keep parents busier than ever as many have a number of extra-curricular activities, which invariably require parental involvement, at the least as a driver. The mantra 'be involved' in your child's life has been well and truly taken up by today's parents.

But has it gone too far? Yes, a good parent is an involved parent, taking part in a child's life. But it can be exhausting working inside or outside the home all week, then devoting all your spare time to your children: driving them to activities, watching them play or perform, or joining in as a coach or assistant. It can leave you very little time for yourself. The idea of having a few spare hours to read a book or laze on the couch is a distant memory for many parents, when life revolved around a partner and friends.

Many parents put their own lives on hold to make the most of the relatively short window of opportunity they have to raise their kids. All power to devoting time to kids, but not at the expense of your own well-being. In this chapter we shall look at some ideas to help you make some space for yourself and your partner, if applicable.

Here's a little test to check out your priorities. Imagine you are a parent with a partner and one child. You have a weekly ration of twelve eggs, which are your only source of protein. How will you ration these eggs?

Here are your choices:

a) Divide them evenly so you each receive four eggs
b) Give six to your child; you and your partner receive three each
c) Give six to your child, four to your partner, with two left for you
d) Take six yourself, give four to your partner and leave two for your child

How did you do?

When I ask parents in seminars to take this test, most opt for choice a – the democratic, sharing model. This is not surprising, as the most common parenting model today is an authoritative model, which promotes equality among family members. Parents often don't like to place themselves too high in the pecking order, so they share the resources evenly.

Choice b is indicative of a child-centric approach to parenting, where the child comes first in most areas of family life. Parents go down this path when they devote all their spare time to their children and neglect to carve out some time for their own interests and activities, or to be with their partner. The trouble with this choice is that kids then easily become egocentric, and they don't learn to take others into account. On a practical level, if you make this choice, you are likely to be so busy relating to each other as parents that as partners you will grow apart. So when the kids leave home, you might easily look at each other, thinking, 'Now what?' So b is not my preferred choice.

If you chose c, you are a devoted parent and partner. No doubt about it. You are looking after your child and your partner really well. People who choose this option generally experience a great deal of guilt as parents, only some of which they can control. They are guilty when their child is unhappy as they must have said or done something to cause it. They are guilty when their partner is unhappy because they are not attending to him or her properly. They feel guilty when they are unhappy because they must be awful to be around. These parents usually put their personal needs on the backburner, so that the other people in their lives can thrive. This is an unsustainable model as, sooner or later, you'll break down, having ensured that those who have become dependent on you can't thrive when you aren't functioning at your usual 110 per cent. C is the martyr's choice and not one I'd opt for.

Okay, that leaves d. That's the one I was hoping you'd choose, but it's the hardest choice for guilt-ridden, relationship-driven parents. Choice d basically says, look after yourself first, devote some of your energy to your partner and then start taking care of your kids.

Most messages coming from the media, schools and parenting experts support the belief that effective modern parents should put their children first, second and third. According to this thinking, those who choose d are bad parents. I think they are sensible parents, who realise that parenting is a marathon, not a sprint, and that those who raise kids have competing priorities, including, perhaps, looking after their own parents. The 'person first, partner second and parent third' model is the best model by far for raising kids. It's the model I'm going to put forward throughout this book to help you raise kids that thrive.

But life doesn't always resemble models. It certainly doesn't work like it does in my test. In reality, most of us would move through the different modes that each choice represents. There are times when kids come first and everything else is put on hold. My own children tended to take a higher priority than normal around exam time, when I would excuse some of their poor behaviour, putting it down to stress, and make sure that most of their immediate needs were met. There are also times when kids' needs should take a back seat to your partner's needs. In my own family, my children and I respected my teacher wife's need for space around school-report time. Certainly I want more personal space from my family during busy times at work.

Healthy families usually adapt to meet the varying demands of family members. However, there will always be a default mechanism that families return to. I believe firmly that the default mechanism by which most families should operate is the 'person first, partner second and parent third' model. Let's explore this further.

2. Work towards a balance

Work–life balance is an overused cliché and an unachievable goal. The term comes out of the late twentieth century, when paid work began to dominate the lives of both genders. It reflects the need for many people to attend to a variety of aspects of their lives other than paid work. These other priorities include family, friends, health and personal wealth.

The notion of the work–life balance is erroneous. The idea that people can somehow attend to many different aspects of life in a balanced way is absurd. We constantly lurch from one area to another, rather than sharing our time equally between a number of spheres. Parents, particularly when their children are in primary school or preschool, spend an inordinate amount of their time either working in a paid or unpaid capacity or attending to their children's needs.

So what do we mean by balance?

Alfred Adler, the father of individual psychology, had a fascinating take on the work–life balance. He claimed that the people who lived the most content, fulfilled lives actively attended to three external factors – family, work and social or community obligations. He maintained that when we neglect one area at the expense of others for an extended period, our general well-being suffers. There is a fourth area that needs our attention and energy as well – our personal well-being. Neglect your physical, intellectual and spiritual well-being and you won't function well in the three external areas.

To be effective as a parent, or in the family, it's important to attend to your work, your social life and your own well-being, including physical fitness and some level of personal interests. This takes prioritising and planning, but first you must give yourself permission to navigate towards a balance and incorporate other areas into your life. Here's the permission: if you do attend to all areas of life, you are likely to become a more effective parent.

You'll be more interesting to be with and have more energy and life to bring to your child-rearing.

Now for the prioritising and planning. I believe balance is something we navigate towards, making continual adjustments along the way. I recommend that you sit down some time and figure out what your priorities are, and then see how close they are to your life right now. You may find that what you say and what you do are miles apart. Some people who say they value their family rarely see them. I've heard people say that their friends are important to them, yet they haven't been to a social function in months. Figure out the amount of time you devote to work, family, social and your personal needs. If you think the proportion of time is right for you then, congratulations, you are achieving what many people only dream about. If you find you want more time for yourself, or that your social life has taken a dive, take some steps to achieve the balance you need. This means you'll have to take some time from one or more areas. If you want more time for exercise, it may mean you have to work a little less, or spend less time driving kids from one after-school activity to the next. That's a tough one. We look at how we can do that next.

3. Take time for yourself

Sounds easy, doesn't it? Take time for yourself. Say it a few times and it'll seem like the most natural thing in the world. The reality for most of us is quite different. I'll be frank. The reality for most women, who are usually the primary parents, is that they are hard-wired to look after the well-being of others. The irony here is that women are more likely than men to look after their physical and emotional health and well-being; however, once they become parents, often their personal life is pushed to one side. Of course, some women have no other option, due to a lack of support networks. Most men neglect their personal health and well-being due to a mixture of 'she'll be right' stoicism and a misguided macho independence, but that's another story.

Taking time for yourself isn't hard. First, you need to work out what you want and what's reasonable at your stage of life. As an empty-nester, time for me includes a leisurely breakfast reading the newspaper with a second cup of coffee. A few years back, when I had kids at home who needed to be driven to school bus stops, such a luxury was out of the question. A quick glance at the head-lines on the sports pages and a few gulps of instant coffee was about as good as it got in the mornings. However, I did manage to eke out some pleasures for myself. Walking the dog each evening was more about giving me a break than making sure the family pooch was exercised.

Maintaining some time for activities that energise and sustain you may happen accidently, but I wouldn't count on it. As our lives get busier, it seems that those who function best are those who put strategies in place to navigate towards a balance. The key strategies to use to achieve time for yourself are: the use of boundaries to protect the activities you want and the ritualising of the behaviours and activities that you value.

Let's look at rituals first. As a busy, work-focused, family-oriented person, I realised some time ago that the only way I could get some time for myself and my friends was to lock in place key activities to make sure they always happened. I am in a social group that meets once a month. I am in a walking group that hits the trails on a fortnightly basis. I love the theatre, so every year my wife and I buy a season ticket to a set number of plays with a group of other people. If it sounds regimented – relax, the rest of my life isn't like that. But these activities have been ritualised so they always happen.

The second reason they always happen is the boundaries I put in place to protect them. Try getting me on a walking day and you'll have no hope as the mobile is turned off and no speaking bookings are made during those days. Try getting me to travel when it's theatre night and you'll find I'm unavailable. I used the same kinds of boundaries when my children were younger. 'Sorry, I can't drive you tonight. You know Wednesday night is my night for –' is the sort of response that my kids have heard from me.

Rituals and boundaries are strategies parents use to make sure the family gets together and to teach kids how to behave. They are also useful strategies to ensure you get some valuable time for the activities that energise you and make you an interesting person to be around. These are great skills to teach your children, too, as one of the legacies of parents who raise their kids to thrive is that they teach them how to live their lives well.

Now let's look at how you can make sure your relationship with your partner stays red-hot and interesting.

4. Make time for your partner and other relationships in your life

When you have kids, you spend a lot of your time relating to your partner as a parent. Many of your conversations revolve around your children – their health, education, leisure and well-being.

You both inevitably become immersed in their lives, you spend less time together with your partner on your own, and when you do you often find yourself talking about the kids. It seems there is always some issue or problem that needs discussing.

It's important to share the load of parenting. I've known many mothers to be sole parents within a dual-parenting relationship, as all the hands-on parenting is left up to them. It's lonely and isolating when you shoulder the parenting alone. Parenting is always more effective when two functioning people work together, sharing ideas, giving each other strength as well as providing a break for each other. The biggest trap for many couples is the failure to maintain their own relationship as people rather than parents. I see it a lot, where couples with very young or primary-school-aged children spend all their time together as a family, while personally they are growing apart rather than together. Aside from their kids, they have little in common. When the kids leave home or become independent, their relationship either needs to be rekindled or inevitably falters. It's better to regularly nourish your relationship than allow it to fall apart due to neglect.

The key is to nurture your relationship in much the same way as you did before your children came along. You may not be able to recapture those times when you spent hours in each other's company, talking about seemingly insignificant matters that opened windows into each other's personalities. But you can recapture some intimacy by building regular 'partner time' into your life.

I suggest you think in terms of regularity, as well as participating in at least one interest you have in common. Keep in mind that strong partnerships recognise and celebrate their past history, enjoy their present lives together and shape their future by working towards shared goals. They have interactions that attend to the past, present and future.

Here are some opinions to consider:

A daily catch-up. Try to spend some time together each day without the kids, when you catch up on each other's day. When the kids are in bed it's tempting for couples to retreat to a book, television or the computer so they never actually catch up and talk about their days. It is easy to fall out of the habit of sharing some of the minutiae of one's daily life, but a lack of regular communication leads to a lack of intimacy and can cause one or both partners to seek solace in someone else.

A weekly or fortnightly rendez-vous. Arrange to meet with your partner on a regular basis to share a coffee, a drink or even a meal. Ideally this should occur outside the house. Change the venue and activity, but try to keep the time constant. The key is to ritualise your rendez-vous. It should be a regular entry in the diary of both partners.

A night or weekend away. Book the kids in with their grandparents or friends for babysitting and make sure you have a night or two with your partner at least twice a year. You don't have to stay in an expensive place. Stay at home if your budget is stretched, and prepare a special meal, or eat out. Try to make the weekend something special for you or your partner. My wife and I have made an art form of nights and weekends away. We began spending a weekend away once a year before our children started school. We'd swap the organising and keep the expectations reasonable in terms of where we went. It was the fact that we got away, rather than the location or surroundings, that we both valued. This grew to two weekends a year and gradually extended to include more extensive travel together as the children have become more independent.

What about sole parents?

Those who parent solo need to get away too. Children can easily become the focus for single parents. This is often more evident in the early days after a separation, when children fill a void left by a partner's departure. Social invitations and offers for assistance can easily be refused and participation in social events can decrease.

Sole parents who are the custodial parents generally get little respite, particularly if your kids are school-aged. It's important for your personal well-being to have a break from your children at least once a week. Not only will kids benefit from having a refreshed parent, but they may appreciate being in the company of someone different. Of course, it's sometimes hard to get away. It helps if you have good support networks. So now I'll look at how to build these.

5. Build your support networks to keep you strong

Some people are natural connectors. They build networks of friends and colleagues easily. These are people who enjoy the company of others and function best when other people are around them. Some people have to work hard at building networks. It's not natural for them to stay in touch with others. They generally need a purpose to contact someone, so when they become busy with work or parenting they can easily become isolated. If networking doesn't come naturally to you, you can still stay in touch with others, you just need to work a little harder to do so.

The most effective parents are those who are surrounded by a group of well-functioning people who have some stake in their lives. Parents quite simply struggle when they are isolated and cut off from their community. The best model for raising children is one in which kids are surrounded by layers of peoples who all have a vested interest in their well-being and the well-being of their parents. In the past this meant extended family, the local church, schools, neighbours and others who were part of a vibrant community. This sense of community isn't as strong in many areas as it once was: churches and schools no longer perform the leadership roles of the past; parents are easily disconnected from extended family due to distance or the busyness of life.

This means that many parents need to be proactive and ensure they have links with strong social groups, as well as professionals who can support them on their parenting journey.

Examine your support network. Do you have access to:

a) A regular babysitter?
b) Someone outside your immediate family to talk about your children with?
c) Someone outside your immediate family to go to for a chat or a laugh with when you feel down?
d) Someone to assist with your mental health?

Do your children have access to:

a) Adults outside their immediate family to talk with if they can't talk to you?
b) Adequate gender models?
c) Mentors (if in adolescence)?
d) Someone to attend to their mental health?

There is no need to stay isolated, as help and assistance is available from many sources, both formal and informal, including: friends, colleagues and family; professional agencies; local councils; schools or preschools; playgroups; before- and after-school care; and different state associations such as the multiple-birth association.

6. Develop a resilience mindset

There are two ways to get fit. You can start a fitness regime, which may include joining a gym, hitting the road to chalk up heaps of kilometres or taking up Pilates, aerobics or one of the many exercise classes available. In other words, you make some big changes designed to bring some immediate results.

The alternative is to develop a fitness mindset and begin to make small adjustments to different areas of your life. Walk to the shops rather than drive. Spend more time in the garden and less in front of the television on weekends. Walk up stairs rather than taking lifts. You won't get the instant results that come from adopting a more serious fitness regimen, but you are more likely to get lasting results over time.

The same approach applies to our mental health and well-being. You can make drastic lifestyle adjustments such as finding a less stressful job, making a sea or tree change, giving up alcohol, taking up meditation. These are the types of changes people make as a result of a health scare or a breakdown of some sort.

Or you can take the gentler approach, adopting a resilience mindset and looking after your mental health and well-being on a regular basis. This is preventative by nature and increases the likelihood that you will stick to the changes you make.

Here are some simple things to do to help you develop a mindset for resilience:

Watch your self-talk. Become more aware of the messages you constantly send yourself. The little voice in your head can have a catastrophic impact on you if you let it. It can talk you into the blues, lower your self-esteem and build mountains out of molehills. Once you are aware of its impact, you can switch it off or change its negative chatter to something a little more positive. Both take practice. It's not as easy as it sounds to alter the patter in your head, but you can work at it.

Watch your language. Build an awareness of your language and its impact on your well-being. You can easily catastrophise about the simplest events so you feel like the sky is about to cave in. If you moderate your language, things won't seem so bad.

Build in regular down time. As a professional speaker I know how easy it is to take bookings for back-to-back presentations week in, week out as the lure of building a healthy bank balance becomes too hard to resist. Working flat-out without a break is a fool's game. I've learned from experience to build regular down time into my schedule, so I can maintain my passion and enthusiasm for my work. When you have a resilience mindset you see the value of down time to your well-being and the positive impact it has on your relationships. You recognise that you smile more and have more energy for the people and activities that you love.

Get plenty of sleep. We are only beginning to make the links between sleep and personal well-being. Mothers of newborns know what sleep deprivation is like. It's debilitating. You can't function properly and you become easily depressed. Many people spend much of their lives experiencing some form of sleep deprivation, and they compensate by taking regular caffeine hits, drinking alcohol and using other ineffective remedies. When you develop a resilience mindset, you'll value sleep more and look for opportunities to get a good night's sleep.

Have something that energises and relaxes you. My dad used to say that everyone needs a hobby. He's right. An interest outside work or family is a boon for your state of mind. Kids generally have few problems in this area, but adults can easily lose sight of the fact that we need to have something in our lives that energises us and makes us interesting.

Stay flexible and realistic in your thinking – don't get locked into 'must do' thinking. Watch your language to see if it's full of absolute, imperative statements such as: 'I must always be on time,' 'They should always use good manners,' 'They never do anything to help.' If this is you, you may be stuck with an inflexible, unrealistic thinking style that causes you a great deal of stress. Catch yourself and wind back your language. 'I must always be on time,' becomes 'I will try to be on time, but sometimes I can't be.' 'They should always use good manners,' becomes 'I would like it if they were well-mannered, but sometimes they aren't.' 'They never do anything to help,' becomes 'They are sometimes helpful but at times they forget.'

If you are not convinced that looking after your well-being is a good idea, I'd like to appeal to an altruistic motive. When you develop a resilience mindset, you get a greater understanding of what resilience is about and are in a far better position to develop a sense of lasting resilience in your kids.

Now let's look at the next part of the puzzle: how you can build a resilient family.

Chapter 2

Build a strong, resilient family

Introduction

Families come in all shapes and sizes these days. A growing diversity of cultural backgrounds, more multiple births, the increase in one-child families and families with a child who has a diagnosed disability have added extra layers to the family construct. (Why are there more kids with disabilities? Because there is more recognition of disabilities. Kids in past generations who may have been labelled as having poor concentration or being behaviourally difficult are now diagnosed with ADHD. Kids who were once considered a little odd with poor social skills are now recognised as having Asperger's Syndrome.)

Regardless of their shape or size, families are a group to which people belong, as well as in which children are born, raised and nurtured. Most children never grow out of their original family. They do, however, grow into a new one, if they form their own family as adults.

The term 'parenting' is a misnomer. It's a twentieth-century term that suggests it takes one or two people to bring up a child. Kids are born into a group, their family. It's a dynamic place with as many relationships as there are members. If there's more than one child then there are sibling relationships to consider. Siblings influence each other in ways that parents can't. The fact that we are born into a family means we have to find our place and learn to fit in. Children are egocentric by nature, but family life means that they need to adjust their wants to fit the needs of others. The child-centric nature of modern parenting, where the child is placed at the centre of events, neglects one of the fundamentals of child-rearing that has served us well over the centuries. That is, the best way to raise kids is to focus on building a strong family, which nurtures them and develops valuable relationship skills for life. It sounds a little scary, but the lessons of family life have always been important to future development.

Effective parenting is about effective leadership; more specifically, the ability of parents to develop a strong sense of 'we' rather than 'me'. Sibling fighting has modern parents tearing out their hair, but parents need to ask themselves: 'Will my children pull together when the chips are down?' Thankfully, the answer is usually a resounding yes, which is a sign of a strong family. Kids may spend a lot of their time squabbling, but they will also fight for their sibling. 'I can fight with my sibling, but you can't' is a healthy notion in many ways.

Effective families are guided democracies or benign dictatorships, in which someone is in charge, hopefully one parent, or two. As parents, what leadership style should we use? We shall look at this next.

1. Create a great family brand

You hear a lot about branding these days. Companies work hard to establish their brands in the public consciousness. Branding is more than just making products and services look a certain way. It is about the image a company projects so that people can make a strong connection with it on an emotional level. Some companies spend a fortune establishing and projecting the right brand. Virgin has been super-successful in doing this. Most people associate Virgin with fun and value for money. Volvo is linked to safety and Mercedes-Benz is associated with prestige.

These associations aren't accidental. They were created purposefully by their corporate governors. They were established as a result of careful thought and reflection on the values the company wanted to represent. Each brand's creators then worked out how those values would be best conveyed to the public through packaging, advertising and marketing. They also made sure there was internal alignment, so that a company actually lived its values. A company that projected a family-friendly image should have family-friendly work practices and work hard to establish a strong sense of community among employees.

Branding is not just for the business world. Families, too, create their own brand. All families project an image of how they function. The image is usually a reflection of the prime values that the parents promote and can also be a reflection of the personalities of family members. Think of any family and, more than likely, you'll be able to sum them up with a few words. I've heard one family described in this way: 'The Smith family is loud and boisterous, but they'd all give you the shirt off their backs.' The Smith family brand may be built around the values of tolerance, fun and generosity. Another family I know was once described as, 'Off the wall, but those kids are so independent and are all doing well in their own way.' The brand of this family may well be independence, fun and a strong work ethic.

Your family brand not only affects how other people see you and what you stand for, but it plays a big part in what sort of adults your kids will become. The predominant values kids learn in their family usually stay with them for life. Those values will be stronger in some children than others, but most children are likely to relate to them.

Family branding is about more than just values, although they are important. The following four aspects contribute to the family brand:

The family atmosphere. What's the atmosphere like in your family? Is it serious or fun? Is it a place where encouragement rules or is it a critical, negative place? Is the atmosphere terrific or toxic? Is it a tense place, where everyone walks on eggshells, or is it a place where humour and relaxation are common? You can impact on your family atmosphere by consciously adopting the mood and mindset you want. If you want an upbeat atmosphere in your family then you can set the tone by being upbeat, positive and enthusiastic.

Shared values and attitudes. What behaviours do you value most highly? What type of kids are you trying to raise? To discover your shared values, step back and look at what your kids have in common. If they are all independent, even your most dependent child, then independence is a shared value. If all your kids are tolerant of others, then tolerance is a shared value. Children's values and attitudes usually reflect parental priorities.

Parenting style. Your parenting style will influence the family frame. For instance, a permissive style, where anything goes, often produces a chaotic family style, where respect for others is lacking. The preferred style that fits today is an authoritative style akin to a guided democracy or a benign dictatorship.

Family rituals and traditions. Rituals and traditions are those habitual, repeatable, unique behaviours that bring you together as a group and identify you as a family.

They include mealtimes, celebrations, birthdays and other traditions unique to your family. Rituals not only anchor your kids to their family but they make quite a statement about what you value. My family, for instance, is BIG on noisy, all-in discussion-type mealtimes, which is reflective of our family as a place to speak out, but to respect others at the same time. In many ways, rituals are icons of family life.

So, take a minute or two to reflect on your family frame. What are the values your kids have in common? Think about the rituals and traditions you are establishing. Reflect on your parenting style and that of your partner. Think a little about the regular family atmosphere. Then try to distil your brand into three or four key words.

One of the obstacles to creating a coherent family brand is a parenting style that is inconsistent, particularly inconsistency between two parents. Next, we will look some ways to overcome these parental differences.

2. Parent together, even when you are not together

A couple approached me after a parenting presentation, asking for my thoughts about kids and mealtimes. One parent was focused on food and was concerned with the quantities their kids ate. The other was focused more on behaviour and the quality of social interactions that mealtimes offered.

From my perspective, mealtimes are more than a mere pit stop for food. They offer a great opportunity for family members to talk while bottoms are anchored to chairs. That's why the TV needs to be turned off when we're eating.

During our brief chat it seemed that both parents respected the other's viewpoint, which was fantastic. But they clearly had some differences in their approach to parenting that may not have been evident before the chat. I suggested they sit down and talk about what they both expected from mealtimes and find a compromise solution that they could both live with.

Differences in parenting approaches are natural, reflecting past experiences as a child and gender differences. These differences are healthy, a sign of independent thinking, and can provide balance to family life. But different approaches can also cause discomfort, stress and anxiety to one or both parents, particularly when communication and empathy levels are down. In some cases, differences can lead to inconsistent parenting, when there is no agreement on rules or standards of behaviour, and inconsistent follow-through when kids behave poorly.

Parents can work together, whether or not they live together. But they need to know when to compromise, when to keep out of the way and when to present a united front. This takes practice and depends on the issues, your parenting styles and your individual values.

There are three levels of partnering:

Level 1 – managerial. This is the day-to-day parenting that focuses on areas such as standards of behaviour, kids' health, education and supervision. Usually one parent (mostly mothers) is the primary parent calling the shots, while the other takes a back seat as the secondary parent (mostly dads). The secondary parent usually follows the lead of the primary parent. Level 1 focuses on WHAT needs to be done to raise kids.

Level 2 – child-rearing. This is a tricky area as it covers approaches to kids' behaviour, how to build confidence in kids, the processes parents put in place for communication and how kids treat others. My conversation with the young couple I mentioned above was around this level. Level 2 fundamentally concerns itself with HOW kids are raised.

Level 3 – values and attitudes. This is the big-picture level. It looks at fundamental things you value such as developing independence, responsibility, tolerance, persistence and respect in kids. These are just a few – there are plenty of values and attitudes to develop. It really helps when partners are on the same wavelength when it comes to the things they value. This level concerns itself with WHY you do the things you do as parents. When you know the WHY then the HOW of parenting becomes easier.

From my experience, you can get away with parental differences when kids are young; however, they do become a big problem as kids move into adolescence. Some teenagers become adept at driving a wedge between parents who are on different wavelengths. They generally go to the parent who will give them the answer they require when it comes to tricky questions such as going out, access to alcohol and relationship issues.

It pays to start the conversation about parenting early on in kids' lives. That's why I love it when a couple comes to a parenting seminar together. They both hear the same message, and hopefully this generates healthy conversations about their kids and parenting. These conversations generally start off around level 2 issues, but involve level 3 issues.

The funny thing is, most parents are so busy talking about level 1 issues that they rarely talk meaningfully about these level 3 issues, which are the absolute guts of what they do. Conversations at the 'why?' level are more fundamental, leading to a greater understanding of where the other person comes from and the likelihood of presenting a united front to kids. And getting on the same page as your partner is always in the best interests of your kids.

Next, we'll look at how to work together with your partner so that you adopt similar approaches to the things that really matter as parents.

3. Work from the same script as your partner

The days of 'go see your mother' are out. Shared parenting is in.

However, if you have a partner, your biggest challenge may be to get on the same wavelength and work from the same parenting script. You may be strict, while your partner is lenient. One of you may value mealtimes, while the other is ambivalent about breaking bread as a family. One may be the fun parent, while the other is the family ogre.

You bring to the job of parenting your own family experiences, as well as the script you inherited from your own parents. The ghosts from the past are strong indeed, and can influence you in profound ways, bringing you into conflict with your partner. As a couple you may be close, but as parents your views and experiences may be a long way apart.

Despite the current shared-parenting rhetoric, most dual-parent families operate on the primary/secondary parent model we've discussed.

Couples tend to vary in how much they share, but rarely is the load split fifty-fifty. Nevertheless, for the sake of family harmony and your sanity it helps if you agree more than you disagree with the way you each parent.

Here are some ideas to help you develop a similar parenting script – i.e. to develop compatible, consistent ways of raising your kids:

Have regular family meetings. If nothing else, meetings, whether formal or informal, force all members of your family to address issues, rules and behaviours as a group. More about family meetings later in this section.

Ask your partner for their opinion. As creatures of habit, we take on roles in families. Break the pattern and ask your partner for advice about the tasks that you normally do, whether it is getting the kids up, dealing with their homework or helping a teen recover from a broken heart.

Bring your partner into the loop. Keep your partner informed about your children's behaviour, educational achievements and general well-being. It is usually the job of the primary parent to update the secondary parent on these issues.

Defer to your partner. As much as is practical, bring your partner into the picture about children's behavioural issues. For instance, rather than continually responding to children's requests yourself, say something like, 'I'm not sure about that. I'll check with your mother/father and get back you.'

Share with your partner insights into your childhood and family, particularly your likes, dislikes and the rituals you enjoyed. Such conversations can lead to a deeper level of understanding and often reveal why you feel strongly about different parenting matters.

Divide areas of responsibility. The art of delegation between parents also means letting go. A hard one for some parents!

Whether you live with your partner or you live apart, one of the greatest gifts you can give your children is the consistency of both parents working together. Consistency between parents also grows from a coherent sense of family tradition. Effective parents ritualise key activities that bring people together and build their own family traditions.

4. Build strong family rituals and traditions

Rituals are the unique family activities or celebrations that bring people together. Strong families build up their own rituals and traditions, which help define them and set them apart.

Birthdays, Mother's and Father's Day, Christmas and bar mitzvahs are just some of the many rituals and traditions that families enjoy. By definition, they are cast in stone and not put aside when life gets busy.

Rituals can also be as simple as a parent saying to a child 'I love you' each day as he goes to school, or the bedtime-story routine that so many children love. The permanence and uniqueness of rituals give them much of their significance.

I've heard Australian psychologist Andrew Fuller describe family rituals as the 'coat hooks upon which we hang our family memories'. This is a lovely turn of phrase that depicts perfectly the importance of family rituals. It is little wonder that when families begin to disintegrate, it is generally rituals that are first to go.

It's strange how teenagers will complain about having to attend family celebrations, yet will be less than pleased if they are cancelled or even changed in some way. Strong family rituals connect teenagers not just to their family but to their childhoods, so teens tend to celebrate birthdays and special days in time-honoured ways well into adolescence and beyond.

Some parents establish rituals to mark their children's stages of growing up. For instance, a child may get a big bike when he is ten and at thirteen have a special meal with both parents to mark the beginning of his teenage years. These rites of passage are fast becoming a feature of many modern families. They also give parents the strength to resist pester power and teach kids that good things come to those who wait.

Perhaps the most effective ritual is that of the family sitting down and eating together. Mealtimes provide the opportunity for people to connect with each other in a meaningful way. They give parents an opportunity to influence their children's thinking as well as to teach them how to be social and sociable. One great way to do this is to promote a strong food culture. Read on . . .

5. Create a strong food culture

For years now, I have been mulling over the notion that countries with a strong food culture generally produce strong families.

A strong food culture is one in which food is valued and enjoyed rather than endured; where food is prepared with care and cooked with some flair, then eaten in a leisurely atmosphere. In such cultures food becomes an expression of love; mealtimes anchor kids to their families and parents don't obsess over every bite a child takes.

In these days of fast food, busy lives and problems as a nation with obesity, it is easy to lose sight of the importance of mealtimes. For these reasons, my wife and I worked hard to develop a strong food culture in my own family. We tried to cook interesting food and present it attractively. We turned off the TV at mealtimes. We insisted that everyone at home came to the meal table, but we didn't insist that every morsel be eaten. Attendance was a non-negotiable, even for busy secondary school students around exam time.

We led the conversation around a variety of topics of interest, hoping the kids would also lead the way when they were old enough. I recall one of my children asking me if there were any gay kids at school when I was young. If so, she wanted to know, how were they treated by their peers? That was a question out of left field that held everyone's attention! We would talk about what we were eating and how it was cooked. This helped the kids learn about cooking and hopefully developed an appreciation of the process, as well as the food itself. One of my children has become a chef, so perhaps all this attention to detail did pay off.

We made sure that everyone helped with some aspect of the meal – either setting the table, cooking, taking away plates or dish-washing. This became part of the ritual of the meal.

American pastor, speaker and author Dr Gary Chapman has developed a powerful relationship model that parents can use to build strong bonds within their family. Chapman maintains that there are five ways to express your love to another person, and we all have our own preferences. The five languages of love are:

- Talking and words of affirmation
- Physical touch and closeness
- Shared quality time
- Gifts and mementoes
- Acts of service

A strong food culture caters to all five points. Shared mealtimes create the opportunity for talking, physical closeness and quality time together. Food carefully, lovingly prepared becomes a concrete, physical gift and an act of service by a parent, and these are the preferred love languages of many kids.

I know food can cause bitter battles between parents and kids. However, there are plenty of behaviour-management strategies to help you turn around mealtimes. Perhaps the best strategy of all is to approach the whole issue from a positive angle. For example, start by having one special mealtime each week, then build from there.

Developing a strong food culture is less about the quantity of shared mealtimes and more about valuing the whole experi-ence, and treating the food and the company as special rather than something to be taken for granted. It is one of the best ways to encourage communication between adults and kids. Here are some more ideas . . .

6. Have more conversations at home

The link between achievement at school and parents' ability and propensity to engage in conversation with kids from a young age is indisputable.

The language stimulation they receive when they talk with their parents is one factor. The language of firstborns is generally richer and more extensive than that of their siblings, who probably spend less time in one-on-one situations with a parent.

But engagement in conversation with parents benefits kids in a far broader sense. It's trite to say that kids learn a great deal from their parents, but they do when we talk with them. Through conversation, kids get a real sense of who we are. By talking with kids we impart some of our knowledge, ideas, wisdom and thoughts, as well as getting a window into how they think.

Starting conversations with kids can be a massive challenge. Busy schedules, homes designed for individual enjoyment rather than group living (in the sense that modern homes have kids-only rooms and parents' retreats) and kids that clam up are some of the obstacles that trip up parents. So you may need to be a little cunning, a little proactive and a little inventive to get some chat going at home.

Here are five ideas to help you get more conversation going in your family:

Turn off the TV (and other screens). Most homes have a range of electronic screens that you compete with to get your kids' attention. Don't be afraid to take control of those screens and create a little conversational space. Start with a screen-free day each week, or a screen-free hour each day if you are a home full of screen junkies.

Turn on the TV (and other screens). If you can't beat them, join them. Some television programs provide great conversational fodder, particularly for older children and teens. This can range from, 'Who's going to win *Australian Idol*?' to 'What happens to the winners of *Australian Idol*?' to 'What is the point of *Australian Idol*?'

Have more mealtimes (with the TV off). The family that eats together talks together . . . or they should. Make mealtimes special and insist that kids sit until everyone finishes rather than that they eat all their peas. Avoid turning mealtimes into food fights that you can't win.

Move more. If sitting and chatting is not your child's thing, try to get them up and moving. Boys will often talk when they walk or play, so consider getting some action happening. When their hands are busy their tongues will often loosen up.

Try shoulder-to-shoulder parenting. Sitting together in a car, washing dishes or playing a game can provide opportunities for talk. Take the eye contact out of the equation and you may find the talk flows more freely with some kids.

Every family has its own way of instigating a conversation. It seems to me that the best communication in families happens when no one is trying too hard, but in busy modern families you probably will need to work hard at it. That's just the way now.

You also need to make sure your conversations don't become interrogations, where kids switch off rather than switch on to what you have to say.

7. Hold conversations, not interrogations, with kids

A few years back, I was really challenged by trying to converse with a young person who was consumed by all the activities she faced in her last year of schooling – study, boyfriend, peer relationships and parties (not necessarily in that order!). My clumsy attempts at conversation were more like interrogations, as I tried to find out what was happening in her life. I needed to stop grilling her and start chatting with her.

But talking involves time, disclosure and respect for privacy. That's a little different from conducting an interrogation. Let's take a look at each of the processes needed for a successful conversation:

> **Take the time to talk.** Busyness is the enemy of effective communication. When conversation happens on the run it tends to be bland and superficial. Daily conversations often don't get past the level on which we try to extract some information about our kids' activities. I'm not sure about you, but I can't stand being asked, 'How was your day?' 'It's still going,' is my usual reply.
>
> Generally, the conversation will reach a level of disclosure when no one is trying to get it to do so. Here's the rub – you have to create little pockets of time and

space when you interact with kids in a natural way and stuff just crops up. Weekends, school holidays, shared interests and games can provide these opportunities. You may have to use some native cunning to create them, but the results in terms of developing a rapport with your kids will be well worth the effort.

Disclose, then listen. Sometimes you have to give a little of yourself to get conversations going. Family mealtimes still offer the best opportunities for conversations, as bottoms are glued to seats, distractions are removed and you can usually talk in a natural way. I have found it useful to get things moving by talking about something different, unusual or funny that may have happened during my day. It is a little like throwing a rope out and seeing who picks it up. Conversation invites reply. Often someone will respond, ask a question, raise an eyebrow, burp, or whatever, and some type of conversation sparks up. If conversation does start then step back a little and listen. Avoid being too analytical or critical. When we interrupt the flow of conversation with our life lessons and parental wisdom, our kids soon learn to stay silent.

Respect their privacy. Modern parents are constantly reminded to take an interest in and be involved in their children's lives. But this doesn't mean we should get tied up in the minutiae. Much of what happens to them on a daily basis is mundane and some of it is none of our business.

Doubtless some readers may think that it would be nice to know even one thing that happens to their kids! Kids will generally choose what to tell you in the same way that we choose what to tell them, our spouses, parents and friends. They are selective with information, and usually will disclose more intimate details when the timing and comfort levels are appropriate.

Now that so much communication between people occurs via an electronic medium of some type, it's easy to forget about the art of conversation. For the most part, conversation is simply a personal communication between people who are interested in each other. We can all do that.

Of course, when there is a little bit of fun in the house, children are likely to be far more open.

8. Have some fun, lots of fun

Members of strong families enjoy each other's company. One way to ensure that people like to be in the company of others is to instil some fun into family life. Having fun has a great deal to do with your attitude and willingness to be playful. It's a good idea to take some lessons from your kids and encourage plenty of play in your family.

Free, unrestricted play is the prerogative of childhood. However, children these days live highly organised, structured lives, so the notion of free play is foreign to many of them.

The importance of play for children is often underestimated. It impacts on all aspects of child development. Outside games develop balance, coordination and fitness. Singing and rhyming games promote language development. Board games and puzzles help intellectual development.

Free play at home is therapeutic for children as well as good for building relationships. Play is an important way that children can express and work through their feelings. They can have plenty of fun on their own, in their bedrooms or a part of the house designated as their own space. When they are young, dress-up boxes, art boxes and other objects and spaces encourage children to use their imaginations and initiative when they play. Older children still enjoy these things, but usually prefer board games and outside games and sports that challenge them and maintain their interest.

Left to their own devices, children generally attend to about the right ratio of work, rest and play – that is, play comes before work and just after rest in most children's scheme of things (just like the alphabetical order). Children generally enjoy playing with their parents as long as they don't always turn play into lessons. The key is to be led by your children and to allow enough time for them to play on their terms.

As a parent, you may need to be proactive and create opportunities for your kids to interact with each other and you on a regular basis. We all can do this in our own way. One dad I know sets up jigsaw puzzles and challenges his family to solve the puzzle within a week. The puzzle is laid out on a table so anyone can sit for a time and add some pieces. Sometimes there is no one there, but at times there'll be more than one child working on the puzzle. Another parent wanting to inject some fun into her family spends a lot of time playing ball games with her kids outside. She doesn't keep a score card, which reduces arguments.

There are plenty of ways to have fun with your kids as a

parent; you don't need a book for ideas. You just need to relax a little, and be willing to inject some levity into your life.

Now for something a little more serious, but very effective, in terms of getting your family to move in the same direction . . .

9. Hold family meetings

At work I'm not a fan of meetings. Too much talk and not enough action is my attitude. But at home I feel altogether different about them. I used regular meetings to give my kids a voice in my own family, as well as to teach them how to resolve some of the conflict that inevitably occurred along the way.

My research suggests that families who have a process for sharing decisions and resolving conflict have more cooperative kids and fewer sibling disputes.

To be truthful, I stopped talking about family meetings in my presentations some years ago, as people's eyes tended to glaze over when I mentioned the M word. But I am now 'talking up' the concept because many parents I have worked with have remarked how useful they were in turning their families around.

In this age of child-centric parenting, family meetings are very relevant. They are a useful way of unifying a family and developing a shared approach to its organisation. They are a great vehicle to move children from being 'me-centred' to 'we-centred'. They are based on the management principle, which recognises that children like a say in how their family operates and are more likely to stick to rules and decisions they have had a say in making than those imposed from above. In many ways, this is stating the bleeding obvious, but we need a process to make it happen. That is where family meetings come in.

Following are ten basic guidelines for conducting family meetings:

They must be regular. Weekly or fortnightly meetings are ideal. If a parent calls a meeting because they want to get some cooperation, then the meetings become a vehicle for Mum or Dad to get their point across, rather than a means for children to participate in family life.

Start when at least one child is five years of age. Children need the verbal and cognitive skills to participate. This varies, but around five years seems to be a good age to start.

Follow a balanced agenda. Share joys and gripes. The meetings will fail miserably if they become a continual whinge session.

Have a chairperson. Initially this should be a parent, but it can be shared around as kids become more competent.

Establish simple rules. Meetings always run more smoothly when there are some common-sense rules to follow.

Start each meeting with encouragement. For example, 'Thanks, Marta, for cleaning your toys away after playing with them this week. It was great have the family room so clean.' This helps set a positive tone and teaches kids how to encourage.

Finish with a pleasant activity. A concluding game or a story will help to reinforce a meeting as an event to anticipate.

They must be real. While meetings should be fun, they are not a game you play with kids. You must be able to live with decisions that are made, so you must be realistic about what is discussed and decided upon.

Short and sharp, not long and dull. Don't allow them to become bogged down. Keep moving them along. A meeting may last only eight or nine minutes, but that's fine if its objectives were met.

It is the process that is important. Sometimes meetings break down in chaos, with no decisions being made. But don't abandon the concept if nothing concrete comes of a meeting or two. The process of meeting and talking is as important as the outcomes.

Regular family meetings are a potent way of improving relationships and building cooperation between parents and children. They provide the means for children to share and accept responsibility, participate fully in family life and work cooperatively for the benefit of the group – their family. In my own family meetings, held for a number of years when the children were in primary school, we discussed personal and family management issues ranging from why the towels were always left on the bathroom floor to how we could assist one of my kids who was having some social difficulties at school. Sometimes the discussion never got off the ground, but more often than not our kids would come up with some terrific solutions. For instance, one asked us to put up more towel racks to solve the towel issue. Problem fixed! As to helping with my child's social difficulties at school, we didn't think up any concrete solutions at the time, but we did engender empathy and sympathy, which was a great support to the child concerned.

Section 2

Building confidence in kids

Self-confidence and self-esteem are inextricably connected. Self-esteem refers to how we feel about ourselves and self-confidence is usually linked to how we act.

Children's self-confidence influences their social behaviour and learning. Children with low levels of self-esteem are less likely to step out of their comfort zones to extend themselves and try new experiences. They tend to take fewer risks than those with healthy levels of self-esteem. Confident kids persist at learning tasks because they know that eventually they will succeed. They experience some anxiety in new social situations, but they either use strategies to overcome their fears, or they take a risk, knowing that they may not be successful.

Quite simply, if children have healthy levels of self-esteem and self-confidence and feel good about themselves, they are more likely to make friends and succeed at preschool and at school.

As I've discussed, levels of self-confidence are influenced by both nature and nurture. Some kids are by their nature greater risk-takers and can separate themselves from poor performance. They don't put themselves down if they fail and are not prone to anxiety in new situations. Neither do they talk themselves out of being successful or having a go. They have self-doubt, but it's not debilitating. Some kids, by their very nature, have lots of spirit.

But the environment a child grows up in influences his or her self-confidence levels. To promote self-confidence you need to provide an environment that is:

Rich in love and time, and supportive of kids' goals.
Kids need to feel loved. They need adults who make time for them and who help them achieve their goals.

Stable and chaos-free. A stable family environment provides the necessary background for kids to develop, grow and take risks.

Opportunity-rich, involving social interactions and self-help skills. Kids need to be exposed to a variety of social experiences with adults and peers so they have plenty of chances to mix and develop their social skills. Similarly, they need plenty of opportunities to do things for themselves at home, at school and in their neighbourhoods.

Psychologically safe – mistakes are not thrown in their face. Children need to grow up in an encouraging environment that allows them to make mistakes without being constantly reminded of them, which creates a fear of failing. When kids fear failure, they act in safe ways to avoid it.

Positive and reasonable in terms of your expectations. Expectations are tricky. Too high and many children will give up. Too low and many will succeed too easily. You need to expect your kids to succeed, not necessarily straightaway, but eventually. Expectations need to be positive and in line with age, stage of development and abilities.

Kids' confidence levels wax and wane, particularly through different stages of development.

Toddlers see themselves through their parents' eyes. They often reflect the confidence levels of their primary parent. Parents need to make their toddlers feel special and loved. Tell them that you love them; avoid giving negative messages and attaching negative labels to them. This gets tricky as, behaviourally, this can be a challenging stage for parents. You need to manage toddlers' behaviour without dampening their spirit or harming their self-esteem.

Three- and four-year-olds can separate themselves emotionally and physically from their parents. They begin to form a picture of themselves and their capabilities separate from their primary parent. They learn about themselves in fairly physical ways, and will begin to compare themselves with others. As parents, you need to mirror to your children that they are capable, and offer a safe, secure, stable environment so they can explore and develop their abilities.

Primary-school-aged children are trying to work out what they can do and how they can fit into their various groups. In many ways, these are prime confidence-building years. Some children's self-esteem falls when they start school, as they meet strange new situations with new peers and new rules. Self-esteem in the primary-school years is often linked to learning, how kids perform at sport, how they get on with others and, later, how they look. Again, as parents you need to reflect back to your kids that they are capable, make the most of teachable moments and help them to work out their strengths.

Adolescent young people have wildly fluctuating confidence levels. Often confidence is linked to hormonal changes: how a teenager looks and how they think they look impacts on their self-confidence. In their teenage years, many young begin to specialise in the areas of life where they experience success, and cease activities at which they don't excel. How they appear in the eyes of their peers is a high driver for many teenagers – positive peer groups impact on their self-esteem. It helps if teens have some practical goals to aspire to and have loving, accepting families to support them.

Birth order also influences kids' confidence levels. Firstborn boys are frequently low risk-takers and can be very self-conscious when young. But eldest girls often have high levels of confidence, particularly in social settings. Younger children sometimes lack confidence when they are small, yet can become risk-taking, high-achieving teens as their older siblings leave the nest. Many youngest kids are risk-takers because they are not as concerned as their older siblings about the approval of their parents.

Knowing this stuff is one thing. Getting inside kids' heads and shifting their thinking is entirely another.

Esteem- and confidence-building is more than developing children's capabilities, since very competent children can be filled with self-doubt. You have to do more than teach them to be optimistic: a Pollyanna-ish feel-good view of the world won't mean children will take risks when they meet real challenges.

So, as parents, you need to tackle a child's lack of confidence on a number of different fronts. Read on to find out how.

Chapter 3

Build resourcefulness and
independence in kids

Introduction

'Am I doing a good job?' is a question we parents constantly ask ourselves. It's worth asking a different (and better) question: 'Am I doing too much for my kids?'

That may sound a little unfair, but it seems that many wonderful, concerned, anxious mums are indeed trying to do exactly that.

There is plenty of information in the media these days to make us feel anxious and guilty as parents. And guilt and anxiety can drive us to do too much for our kids.

Consider the following questions:

1. Are you your children's home entertainment machine, constantly occupying them, or do you give them sufficient opportunity to keep themselves amused?
2. If a child says, 'I'm bored,' do you believe it is your job to occupy them, or do you see this as an invitation for them to use their own initiative, imagination and creativity?
3. Do you do most of the jobs around the house, or do your kids have assigned jobs and chores, even if they are very young?
4. Are you currently making yourself redundant, or are your kids becoming more dependent on you to look after them?
5. Do you spend a great deal of your time taking your kids to activities outside their normal school/preschool/child-care activities, or is there plenty of down time, when they can just muck around?
6. Do you see it as your responsibility to resolve your children's disputes, or do you give them opportunities to work out their conflicts themselves?

7. Do you assume personal responsibility for your children's eating, choice of clothes and homework, or do you believe that these are issues they need to take responsibility for?

Okay, these questions assume that life is black and white and that parenting is an either/or proposition. Granted, it is never quite as simple as it may be presented in these questions.

However, it is worth considering that for the right reasons you may be doing a little too much for your children. Your job as a parent and as a mother (and father) is to step back and allow your children into the frame.

When we move towards redundancy, our children naturally move towards resilience and resourcefulness. That is the goal of effective (and exceptional) parenting. Now let's see how we can make this magic happen.

1. Do less so kids do more

Redundancy is your goal! I am not talking about becoming redundant in an emotional sense; rather that you need to make your children less reliant on you by developing their independence.

It's easy for parents to take on the jobs and responsibilities that really should belong to our children. With toddlers, it is so easy to dress, feed and clean up after them rather than giving them these jobs. With school-aged children we can find ourselves making lunches, getting them out of bed and cleaning out their school bags, rather than handing these basic tasks of living to them. And we pay for teenagers' mobile phone bills, drive them when there is public transport available and forget to ask them to help out at home.

Tip number 1: be clear about who owns jobs or tasks in your family and don't take on a child's job, or part of a task, unless there is an extenuating circumstance such as illness.

I recently met a mother who was very clear about the allocation of jobs in her family. It is her job to wash the clothes of her early teenage children, but it is their job to place them in the washing basket. She doesn't check bedrooms as it is not her job to place kids' clothes in the washing basket.

Okay, I can hear you thinking, 'Sounds good, but what happens if her kids don't give a toss about being dirty?'

Good point. This mum has a son who does neglect his personal hygiene. But she doesn't become overly fussed about it. She certainly didn't get fussed when he played a game of football in the same wet, muddy jumper that had lain in his sports bag for a week. And she happily showed him how to work the washing machine when he wanted to wear his favourite shirt but had forgotten to put it in the washing basket.

Tip number 2: never be more worried about a child's job than they are, otherwise it becomes your job again.

This mum remained very clear that it was her job to wash the clothes but it was not her job to remind her kids to put their clothes in the washing basket. She knew that as soon as she reminded them, it became her job again.

Here's my challenge for you: think of a job that you regularly do for your child, which he or she could do for him- or herself. Then step back and enable your child to do that job for themselves on a full-time basis. Do less, not more, for your kids.

2. Make sure kids help at home . . . without being paid

Confident kids are competent kids. Past experience has taught them that they can be successful. One way to help develop a sense of competency is to give kids opportunities to help out at home. There is no need to overburden children with jobs, but a sensible allocation of chores according to their age, study requirements and interests is not only a great help to you, but good training for them. They develop both the skills of independent living when they help at home, and the notion that they are capable.

It's best to expect children to help without being paid. By all means provide them with regular pocket money, but avoid linking it to chores. Doing chores in exchange for money develops in children a notion of 'What's in it for me?', which is a self-centred view of life.

Many parents have difficulty getting their children to help. Rather than continual nagging or even giving up asking them to help, keep your expectations high and put some of the following strategies in place to encourage your child to help out at home:

Keep it real. Kids can sense when parents are giving them jobs simply to keep them busy. Make sure the jobs you apportion make a real contribution to the family's well-being.

Balance personal chores with family jobs. Chores are generally divided into two areas. Jobs such as keeping a bedroom tidy benefits a child and jobs such as setting the table benefit the family. By doing both, kids learn to contribute positively to family life.

Place the more arduous or difficult tasks on a roster. The children can refer to it when needed, which takes the load off you and removes the need to remind them. Rotate unpleasant tasks frequently.

Use Grandma's principle to make sure jobs are done. Grandma's principle is to do less pleasant tasks first. That is, make sure jobs are finished before mealtimes or before starting pleasant activities such as watching television.

Avoid doing jobs for children. This is tricky. When you do children's jobs for them, you are in effect taking away their responsibility to do them. It's better in the long run to leave their allocated jobs for them, even if that means some inconvenience. For instance, you may choose not to cook a meal one night until the dishwasher has been unpacked, which is one of your children's jobs. Some-times a little short-term pain needs to be experienced by everyone for some long-term gain.

Show your appreciation for their help. Make a fuss when they help so they know that their contribution to the family is valued. If you do it often enough, they may even show their appreciation for all you do for them!

Keep your standards high. Don't accept half-hearted efforts or half-completed jobs. If you think your child is capable of putting the cat food back in the fridge and placing the spoon in the dishwasher, then insist that he or she does just that, rather than leaving the cat food on the side and the spoon in the sink. A job properly done is valued in the world of work, which they will eventually enter.

Rebrand the term 'chore' as 'help'. The term 'chore' definitely has an image problem. Use the term 'help' – it is easier on the ear and really does indicate what you want from your kids.

3. Teach kids the skills to be independent

There are many aspects to being a parent, but one of your fundamental roles is to be a teacher. In fact, effective parents spend a lot of time with their kids teaching them something. But when we get really busy, it's often easier to do things ourselves – we've talked about the 'Velcro' effect.

We short-change our kids by taking short cuts, or doing things for them. Teaching and training need to be part of the everyday repertoire of a parent. This means we need to add a little extra time to our interactions to help our kids acquire some of the basic skills of living, whether it is a young child learning to do up his or her shoelaces, or a teenager learning how to fill out a tax form.

Here's a simple model I use to teach kids a range of skills, from making a bed to cooking a meal or completing a tax form:

- You watch me.
- You help me.
- I'll help you.
- I'll watch you.

If you want a child to learn to make a bed, ask them to watch you making their bed. Then get them to help you to make their bed. The next time, help them to make their bed, and finally stand back and give them the task to do on their own. Of course, it's easier if you start this process when children are very young – before they start school, when they are malleable and want to help. The same principle holds for developing responsibility in kids.

4. Give kids real responsibility and real problems to solve

Most parents want to develop responsibility in their kids. It's a no-brainer really! But how do you do it? My youngest daughter's preschool teacher taught me many years ago. My daughter was four at the time. One morning at preschool, the teacher met her in the foyer and asked her to put her library book in the library bag. As quick as a flash Sarah said, 'Daddy forgot to pack it!'

The preschool teacher promptly replied, 'Sarah, I didn't ask Dad. I asked YOU!' Good point. This smart teacher thus gave Sarah the responsibility of bringing her book to school each day.

The teacher then gave me a great piece of advice, which I've been following ever since. She glared at me and said, 'Your job as a father is to make it easy for her to remember, but not to take the responsibility away.' So I reminded Sarah after reading her book each day to place it by the front door so she'd remember it on the way out. But it was up to Sarah to put it in her bag on the way out.

Sometimes she forgot. So her teacher would growl and I would stand back.

This simple scenario has repeated itself in hundreds of different ways with all my children. There have been many times when I have had to stand back and allow them to take responsibility for aspects of their lives. Often they've messed up, but then it's been my job to support them emotionally and in any other way, and help them to learn from the experiences.

However, it's all very well developing independence and problem-solving in safe situations. But what about when kids want to stretch their wings and move a little bit further?

5. Build scaffolds to independence

As parents, we will eventually confront a situation in which our child wants to do something that we consider risky or not within their capabilities. For example, your seven-year-old son asks to go into a public toilet on his own. Your six-year-old daughter asks if she can make herself a cup of tea. Or your twelve-year-old daughter wants to catch a train into the city to watch a movie with her friends.

These are tricky parental dilemmas. On one hand, you want to develop a sense of independence in your kids. You should welcome their willingness to have a go. On the other hand, your duty of care means you must assess whether your child will be able to manage the potential risk attached to a situation.

A variety of factors influence our decisions to grant kids independence. These include birth order: parents are often more protective of firstborns than their younger siblings. Our own childhood experiences influence us: overprotective parents often beget overprotective parents. And assumptions about gender competence have a bearing on our views: our beliefs about the maturity levels and capabilities of boys as opposed to girls may differ.

Many parents underestimate their children's abilities, while children often overestimate them. This is a common problem with parents of teenagers – a fourteen-year-old thinks she is three older than she is, and her parents think she is three years younger. So, finding some middle ground is imperative.

There is little doubt that modern parents are an anxious bunch. Caring we may be, but daring we are not. Letting go and granting kids sufficient space is perhaps our greatest challenge.

So how do you grant kids greater independence when there is an element of risk involved? The solution is to build scaffolds. That is, to look for opportunities to move your children closer to independence while keeping them safe.

Here are three ways you can build scaffolds to independence for your child:

Look for simple, safe options to start. Allowing your son to go to the public toilet on his own at the local swimming pool is easier and safer than in a large shopping centre.

Do activities together. Making a cup of tea with your daughter is great way to teach her about safety.

Break complex activities into simpler activities. Catching trains with friends on short trips is good practice for kids who are itching to do some activities with friends without parental supervision.

If your impulse is to respond with 'No! Wait until you are older' when your kids ask for greater freedom, think instead about looking for opportunities to move your child further down the road to independence in small steps. Building these scaffolds to independence is one way you can move towards redundancy while ensuring that your kids stay safe. Sometimes kids will mess up, or experience outcomes that are less than pleasant. How do you react as a parent when your kids experience difficulties? Next, we will look at how to turn negative experiences into valuable opportunities for learning.

6. Make the most of teachable moments

When kids experience hardships, frustrations and difficulties, we just want to take away their pain. But when we focus solely on making the situation better, we miss some first-rate opportunities to help our kids learn and grow.

Problems can be big learning opportunities. Most commonly such problems are: change, loss, rejection, failure, disappointment and conflict.

Perhaps your child has experienced one of these common challenges:

- Being taught by a less than favourable teacher
- Being snubbed by a classmate or friend
- Being left out of a team, even though they tried hard
- Worrying about going to school camp
- Having something stolen from them

I am not suggesting that we want bad things to happen to our kids, but life throws up these types of curveballs all the time. How well they cope will be determined by their resilience and the mindsets of the significant adults around them.

When parents and teachers have mindsets for resilience, they see these situations as teachable moments. A teachable moment is easily missed when we focus on the problem in the present.

When faced with a teachable moment, ask yourself:

How can I teach my child to cope? Encouraging your child to talk about problems, such as the teacher he or she doesn't get on with, is a great coping skill.

What can my child learn about himself for next time? A child may learn when he goes on a school camp he was dreading that he can spend time away from home and still survive.

What can my child learn to avoid or turn around this situation? A child may learn that he can reduce conflict with less pleasant peers by ignoring nasty comments and actively spending more time with friendly kids.

Parenting has always required an exceptionally strong set of skills, including caring, nurturing and negotiating. That's why it is such a hard job. But the longer I am involved in parenting, the more I am convinced that it is fundamentally about teaching. The ability to pass on skills, knowledge and attitudes is the most important skill of all. We teach by modelling, but we also teach kids explicitly. That means we talk to kids about 'stuff' and help them work out how they may cope with or manage different situations they meet.

Mastering teachable moments is how parents help their kids

become resilient and bounce back from some of the setbacks they encounter now and, importantly, in the future. And there's something else you can do to help your kids succeed . . .

7. Promote persistence in kids

Imagine that at the birth of your child you are given a choice between bestowing great intelligence or great persistence on your baby. Which would you choose?

Take your time and think about it! Your choice would impact heavily on your child's success at school, their future levels of achievement and, eventually, their income levels as an adult. The ability to persist at a task and see it through to the end is one of the most important attributes that you can develop in a child.

There are numerous times every day when children must persist rather than give in. A toddler learning to tie shoelaces must persist. A primary-school student must show determination to finish tasks and a secondary student needs to solve problems, particularly those he doesn't understand right away. They need to be able to persist when work gets hard or life gets tough. They need 'stickability'.

What does a persistent child do? Persistent kids do some or all of the following:

- They stick at tasks until the end.
- They set goals and work towards them.
- They focus on tasks and are not easily distracted.
- They don't let failure stop them.
- They are more likely to take risks as learners.
- They can be seen as stubborn or unwilling to bend.

Some children are more naturally predisposed to persist than others. They have a determined, even competitive, streak in their temperament that doesn't allow them to give in. They can drive themselves very hard to succeed.

However, the results of the Australian Temperament Project show that persistence is the temperamental factor that can be improved most over time. Parents and teachers can develop persistence in children. But they can also impede its development by making life too easy for children.

Parents can be a sounding board for children's gripes, but they should show confidence in their kids' ability to cope and get through their difficulties, as Jack's father did at the beginning of the book. 'You can do it' is far more powerful in terms of promoting an attitude of persistence than, 'If it's a little too hard, try something else.'

Let children know that there is a correlation between effort and success. They need to learn that by exerting themselves, they are likely to experience more success. The ability to persist in the face of difficulties is one of the best attributes a child can develop.

Here are five practical strategies you can use to promote sense of persistence in your child:

Model persistence on a daily basis so your child sees what it is.

Develop a vocabulary for persistence. Phrases such as 'hang tough', 'work hard' and 'hang in there' can become part of your everyday vocabulary.

When a child sticks at a task, point it out to them. Make it clear when they have been persistent; that way they will see that it generally pays off.

Help children to remember times when they experienced success by hanging in.

Talk about hard work with your children. They must understand that to be successful they need to do things that are not fun or easy. While it would be good if all work and learning was fun, in reality this is not the case.

Kids can practise persistence in many forums, including at school, or behaviourally, when they keep at you to buy them something. That type of persistence we can do without. But there is another way kids can develop persistence and work towards goals such as becoming independent.

8. Encourage hobbies to build independence

Does your child have a hobby? Does he or she have an interest that is a little left field, such as collecting things, keeping chooks or making model aeroplanes? If so, they are developing some valuable life skills that may not be taught at school.

Some time ago I listened to a well-known businessman tell his life story. It was a typical rags-to-riches, pull-yourself-up-by-your-bootstraps tale. This well-known figure left school at twelve, because he didn't fit the traditional academic environment. However, he explained that as a child he had a number of different hobbies, which enabled him to experience success, feel like he was in control and learn a range of organisational skills. What were these amazing hobbies? He bred and sold dogs. He collected and swapped stamps. He made model aeroplanes and joined a club where he flew them each Sunday.

The skills he learned from these hobbies set him up for life. His breeding venture taught him valuable business skills, including the basics of profit and loss, marketing and bookkeeping. His stamp collecting taught him the value of marketing and networking. Through his interest in model aeroplanes, he learned the value of sticking to a task until it was finished. And as he was shy person, the communal nature of his model-aeroplane club brought him into contact with like-minded souls and he learned to make friends for the first time.

His experiences were a fascinating testament to the value of hobbies and interests developed in childhood. I wonder what skills this entrepreneur would have learned if he'd sat in front of a television, a games console or even a computer when he got home from school each night.

Kids need at least one interest outside school. Having a hobby helps them to relax and become absorbed in something apart from school or home routines, which is good for their mental health. As we've discussed, anxiety seems to be quite an issue these days with many kids, so the opportunity to lose themselves in an enjoyable activity away from the pressures of school has become even more important.

Every child needs to be good at something. Because young people from the age of about thirteen tend to define themselves in terms of what they excel in, it's important that they find a niche. If they don't experience success at school, then hobbies and outside interests become crucial.

Of course, kids can have too many interests and be too busy. I have known children who have a different after-school activity for every day of the week, which leaves little time for homework, family time and reflective time. Like everything in life, achieving a balance is important.

Many kids opt for a sport as their outlet, but not every child or teenager enjoys sport. As a parent it's important to help your child develop a hobby that suits them, and it doesn't matter if it's not part of the mainstream. It may be necessary to encourage your child to try different hobbies as it takes some experimentation to find out what they like and what they are good at.

And there's another great way to develop independence . . .

9. Use pocket money for independence

'How should I give my children pocket money?' is one of the most common questions asked at parenting seminars. 'Should kids receive pocket money when they complete jobs and should they lose it if they are poorly behaved?' are also common queries.

Giving pocket money is an excellent way to develop independence in children and young people. Children should receive their small share of the family wealth, just as they should share the workload at home. For this reason I prefer not to link pocket money to chores or behaviour. This is not to say that the family income should be divided equally between all members. Rather, children are given a realistic sum of money that accounts for their age, needs and ability to deal with it.

Here are five ideas to help you use pocket money to develop independence and a sense of generosity in your children:

Give pocket money regularly. Like adults, children should have a payday each week or fortnight, when they receive their share of the family wealth. My children received their pocket money at the conclusion of our family meetings. This was not so much a reward but a way of helping me remember to pay them. (I do suspect, though, it may have been a factor in the success of our meetings!)

Use the 'three jars' concept. Provide three jars for children when you give them pocket money – one for spending, one for saving or investing and one for charity. Ask children to distribute their pocket money among the jars. Giving children coins rather than notes makes this activity easier. This is a fascinating activity, which gives you the chance to teach kids a great deal about money and its use. For instance, you can get across the idea of saving rather than spending. You can also introduce them to the notion of tithing, or setting aside some of your income for charitable purposes. You may want to have a rule that once money is allocated to a jar it cannot be retrieved later!

Link pocket money to age, stage of development and needs (not wants). Provide your children with guidelines about spending, including what they are expected to buy with the money you give them. A child in preschool and lower primary school may get enough to purchase some sweets and one or two other items, whereas a child in upper primary school may get enough to cover lunch orders, bus money and some treats. An allowance that covers clothing can be useful for adolescents, who can be very costly to outfit.

You can pay me back later. If you get sick of your children asking you for treats or the latest fad or gadget, suggest that they make a purchase or at least make a contribution from their personal wealth. If you are pestered at the supermarket to buy an ice cream or some such treat, you can say, 'Certainly you can buy an ice cream. If you haven't any money with you, I'll buy it and you can pay me back when we get home.'

Teach children about goal-setting. By encouraging children to save for or contribute to a big-ticket item such as a bike or skateboard, they learn a great deal about planning and looking ahead, the value of budgeting and they experience the personal satisfaction of reaching a goal.

When used wisely, pocket money is a great way to develop independence in children and young people. And, by the way, it may be smart to cut or reduce allowances when your kids turn fifteen and encourage them to get a part-time job so they begin to pay their own way.

Now, it's all very well developing your children's independence in the offline world, but kids these days spend so much time online . . .

10. Go online safely

Kids use the internet like their parents used the telephone. They use it for entertainment, education and communication, and not necessarily in that order. In some ways chat rooms are the milk bars and hamburger joints of today – places where young people can spend time without adult interference. The net itself is not to be feared, but it can distort reality if your young person spends all their waking hours online.

The much-publicised risk of predators is small compared to the risks associated with excessive use and the consequent isolation. While the research about the effects of the net on children and young people is thin on the ground, it is fair to say that many concerns arise from overuse at the expense of offline activities and relationships.

The internet has myriad attractions for young people. It is instantaneous, interactive and immensely private, which are highly prized attributes for most young people. It gives them access to their mates, music and media without leaving home. It has addictive qualities, though they don't mean that a young person will become a net addict.

So how should parents react to their children's use of the internet?

Treat dot-com relationships and activities like any other. Mocking their online friends and activities can only drive your kids further into the cyber world. But if these are the only relationships a child or young person has, the alarm bells should be ringing. It is also useful to point out that online friends are not necessarily real friends.

If the online world is the real world for your young person because he shuns most other activities, as well as people, it's time to take some action or get some help.

Involve yourself in their online activities, much as you would any other type of activity. Take the time to find out what they are doing and what they get from it. While you want to give kids space, issues such as internet safety warrant close checking.

Negotiate time allocations to make sure online time is shared with other interested siblings. Locate the computer connected to the internet in a public part of your house so that it can be used by everyone and you can keep an eye on what's going on.

Ask your young person what is a reasonable amount of time online. If they continually violate that limit, or choose a very high number of hours, they may have a problem. Let them think it over. Consider bargaining real-time activities in exchange for time online.

Suggest offline alternatives to online entertainment, education and communication. Remind them that there are offline alternatives, even if they don't use them all the time.

The internet offers many opportunities for young people to connect with each other and stay informed. It can be a very positive thing; however, it is healthy to maintain a balance between online and offline activities and relationships. Without being too pushy, try to ascertain what your children use the internet for and set some limits for its use, much as you would for the use of the television.

Chapter 4
Build kids' self-esteem

Introduction

Self-esteem is a greater predictor of a child's success than intellectual ability or natural talent. Numerous studies support this notion. For instance, a longitudinal study by the London School of Economics Centre for Economic Performance followed the fortunes of all babies born in a particular week in Britain. There was clear evidence that children with higher self-esteem at the age of ten had greater earning power later in life than those with higher maths, reading and other academic abilities. The study found that 'high self-esteemers', as it called them, had less chance of being unemployed later in life and, if they were, they would soon be back in the workforce.

Parents and teachers intuitively know that feelings of self-worth and positive self-esteem are important. But what is self-esteem and how do you know if your child has healthy levels of it or not?

Self-esteem is a realistic and optimistic view of one's value; the favourable or unfavourable attitude you have of yourself. If a child evaluates him- or herself positively and sensibly, rather than negatively and unrealistically, they are usually deemed to have healthy self-esteem.

Most of the research available tells us that children with healthy self-esteem do the following:

1. **Take reasonable risks.** They will try new tasks even if success is not assured.
2. **Display favourable attitudes to others.** Children with healthy self-esteem don't need to put down others to feel competent.
3. **Generally behave well.** They do not have to find their place in their family or in groups through misbehaviour.

4. **Highlight their own strengths, successes and skills.** They don't put themselves down, nor do they exaggerate their own skills or successes to gain a sense of superiority.

5. **Downplay and accept mistakes, failure and imperfections.** They don't dwell on mistakes or failure. Mistakes are part of learning – just ask any golfer.

6. **Are willing to try; show initiative.** Conversely, children with low self-esteem give up easily or show little confidence in areas that are new.

7. **Acknowledge their own contributions.** They take realistic credit for their successes without being boastful or saying that an achievement was due to luck.

8. **Compare themselves to similar children or young people, not glossy images.** It is natural and healthy to compare yourself to others, but the choice of yardstick is critical. Those with low self-esteem tend to use unrealistic figures as a yardstick for success.

9. **Have a positive outlook and use positive language.** Take note of the language a child or young person uses. Healthy self-esteemers know how to positive-track or reframe negative situations into a positive.

10. **Believe that personal limitations can be worked on.** Children with healthy self-esteem know that success is linked to effort. That is, hard work is no guarantee of success but it certainly increases its likelihood.

In the past, it was thought that we could enhance self-esteem simply by making children feel good about themselves. This is too simplistic. The building blocks of self-esteem are multi-dimensional and include the following four aspects:

1. Positive parent, family and teacher interactions and expectations
2. Positive peer interactions
3. Coping skills
4. Successes that show competence and mastery

Parents need a range of skills and strategies to help children develop healthy self-esteem and maintain it, even when events conspire to really challenge them.

1. Kids soak up your language, and your thoughts

You have a great opportunity to influence the mindsets and thinking of your children in positive ways. Consider the impact your parents' repeated messages have had on your thinking. Sometimes I think I am channelling my father. I open my mouth and his words leap right out. I've heard myself using his exact words and tone of voice when I talk to my kids. It's frightening!

It's not just his words, but many of my dad's attitudes I hear. Some are fantastic and have set me up for life: 'Hard work never hurt anyone,' 'Never say a bad thing about someone else that you wouldn't want to hear said about yourself,' and 'If it's worth doing, it's worth doing well,' rattle around inside my head and continue to resonate with me.

Other thoughts and comments are not so helpful. For instance, 'Money doesn't grow on trees,' is one of his homilies I am constantly fighting. To me it reflects a scarcity mindset rather than an abundance mindset, but that is a topic for another time.

These throwbacks to one's parents' thinking occur spontaneously and continually in any of the hundreds of interactions that parents have with their kids each week. They occur when families simply sit around the kitchen table shooting the breeze.

Kids pick up information everywhere. TV, friends and teachers constantly bombard them with all sorts of slogans, phrases and supposed wisdom. But it is the language of parents that has the greatest and most lasting impact. Parents have two advantages in this way. First, we have the advantage of repetition. We spend more time around our kids than others do. As we are creatures of habit, we tend to say and do the same things over and over. Second, parents are the most significant adults in their kids' lives, which make us more influential than other people. Admiration and repetition, when combined, are potent influencers.

Our children absorb many messages without us even knowing it. What sort of messages do your kids hear from you?

Do they hear **'You can do it'** messages, or do they hear 'That's a bit beyond you' messages?

Do they hear **'Life's exciting and full of opportunity'** messages or do they hear 'Life's a bitch and there isn't much you can do' messages?

Do they hear **'Be friendly to others'** messages or do they hear 'Look after number one' messages?

American psychologist and author Martin Seligman made what I think is one of the most significant parenting discoveries of the twentieth century whilst doing his ground-breaking optimism research. During the 1980s and early 1990s, he found that by the age of eight, children usually explain the good things and bad things that happen to them in comparable ways to their mothers. He called it 'explanatory style'. I prefer to call it a 'mindset' – an automatic default way of thinking. As young children tend to be in their mother's company the most, it is their mother's mindset they are most likely to adopt. Seligman's finding is counter to the current notion that media and friends, rather than parents, have the greatest influence on kids.

Australian-based psychologist Michael Bernard found that confident kids have three automatic mindsets. They are:

Self-acceptance. 'If I make a mistake, it doesn't reflect on me. I am still okay.'

Risk-taking. 'Nothing is gained without taking on some challenges.'

Independence. 'I am responsible for my own thinking and behaviour. No one else is.'

Think of some phrases you can use with your kids that reflect these mindsets and start making them part of your language. Do so well and often enough and you will find that your kids' thinking will start to default to self-confidence rather than self-doubt. But you have to believe it can happen.

Some children will be reluctant to extend themselves, regardless of your messages. Most often it's not laziness but fear of failure that holds them back. The strategy that's most valuable to you when it comes to such an issue is to . . .

2. Encourage kids to take risks

Encouraging children to step out of their comfort zones to extend themselves and take risks is one of the great modern challenges of parenting.

Toddlers tend not to be risk-averse or fazed by failure. However, something happens as they get older and become aware that others judge them according to how well they perform rather than how much they try. Firstborn children in particular are risk-averse, with tendencies to stick to tried-and-true activities so they won't make mistakes or errors.

'If I don't make an error, my self-esteem stays intact,' is the attitude of many reluctant risk-takers. This attitude prevents them from making the most of the opportunities that are presented to them in and out of school.

There are two basic strategies you can use to encourage kids to take more risks:

Help children experience success in activities that require a small risk. Kids will take risks if they think their chances of success are reasonable. This means adults need to be careful with their expectations and to structure activities so the likelihood of success is tipped in children's favour, particularly early on in a learning process.

When kids experience success in small risk-taking activities, they are more likely to take bigger risks next time. For example, a child may resist giving a talk in front of the whole school if he has little experience of speaking in front of groups. However, if he successfully gives some talks in front of smaller groups, he is more likely to take the risk of speaking in front of a large group. Small successes breed confidence.

Give kids a pat on the back for taking risks. Regardless of the result, give kids a pat on the back for taking a risk when failure or errors were likely to result. And don't get too upset by their failures, otherwise they will learn to stick to safe options just to please you!

3. Encourage more, praise less

In the last few decades, parents in many parts of the world have enthusiastically followed the positive parenting path, constantly showering children with praise. But for some, giving praise for a job well done has become a sort of nervous tic:

> 'You finished your meal. What a guy!'
> 'That's the best work I've ever seen!'
> 'You are such a brilliant little swimming girl.'
> 'You used the toilet. Let's ring Grandma and tell her what a clever girl you are!'

Most parents are well aware of the importance of praise, but are we going too far? Parents and teachers can praise children so much that it rolls like water off a duck's back, and lacks any real meaning.

Children gain their self-esteem from the messages they receive and through their interactions with the world. The main developmental tasks for under-tens are to work out what they can do and how they fit into the world. 'Am I a chump or champ?' is a question that concerns many children.

Praise has been promoted as the predominant parental tool to boost children's self-esteem. But, like any tool, it can be overused so that it becomes ineffective. Too much praise can be *demotivating*. If a child is told everything he does is FANTASTIC, how will he ever know when he has done something that really is fantastic? Sometimes the mundane and mediocre need to be recognised for what they are, rather than boosted to another level.

Also, the more we praise some kids, the more they expect it. And they soon become addicted to praise. If they don't get a regular fix, they wonder what's wrong.

Encouragement is a far more powerful esteem-building tool than praise, and it doesn't have the adverse side effects. The differences are slim but important. Encouragement focuses on the process of what a child does, whereas praise focuses on the end result. Encouraging comments focus on effort, improvement, involvement, enjoyment, contribution or displays of confidence, whereas praise concerns itself with good results.

An encouraging parent gives children feedback about their performance, but ensures the feedback is realistic and works from positives rather than negatives. An encouraging parent will note a child's efforts in, say, toilet-training and recognise that mistakes are part of the learning process, so they are not too fussed about the results. Praise, however, is saved for a clean nappy and a full potty.

Encouragement recognises that a child is participating in and enjoying a game, while praise focuses on winning or a fine performance. Okay, the differences are academic and it may seem like splitting hairs, but the results on the potty, in a game or even at the kitchen table should not concern adults more than they do children.

As soon as we become more concerned about results than our children are, we take the responsibility away from them. In short, praise is about control and encouragement is about influence.

Praising and encouraging kids can be difficult for many people. Some are simply hard-wired to criticise rather than praise. Fortunately, encouragement is a skill that can be learned. To be effective, it needs to be applied consistently. Encouragement and positive expectations go hand-in-hand. Parents who encourage their kids expect them to succeed – though not necessarily straightaway, and not necessarily with ease. Such parents recognise that kids will be anxious at times, but they have faith in their ability to cope. They also value their kids as they are, not for who they hope they are going to be.

Here are four ways to encourage kids:

Practise empathy and show faith in them. Parents need to recognise their children's genuine anxieties and fears, but also demonstrate faith in their ability to cope. When parents give their kids real responsibilities, from handing in a note at school to being home on time as a teenager, they are indicating they have the ability to handle responsibility, self-regulate and be independent. If parents discover their faith is not warranted, they need to renegotiate the guidelines with their kids.

Recognise effort and improvement. It's easy to recognise jobs well done, such as winning a contest, earning a badge at school or making a bed really well. But what do you do with kids who struggle in areas important to them and you? Focus your comments on effort and improvement. Help them to set realistic goals in line with their capabilities and interests. Learning five new spelling words a week may be more realistic than the twenty words that the school may require.

Focus on strengths and assets. Fault-finding can become an obsession for parents, particularly when they have teenagers. Some kids have strong traits, which at first seem like liabilities. Kids who are determined to have their own way may seem rebellious and stubborn. They can be labelled as difficult. But these qualities and behaviours have a positive side. Dogged determination to succeed is a valuable asset in any field of endeavour and is usually applauded. Rather than criticise, step back and recognise the value of such characteristics. Similarly, focus on the interests and abilities that children possess rather than things they can't do. If music is their forte rather than academic success, don't focus on where they come in their maths class. Celebrate their beautiful piano-playing instead. Often when we focus on kids' strengths, assets and abilities in certain areas, they improve in other areas as well. Confidence has a snowball effect.

Accept mistakes and errors. We live in a society that celebrates success and achievement. Perfect marks, immediate results and getting things right are highly valued. We forget at times that mistakes are part of life. We tolerate errors in adults, but often we don't in children. View errors as valuable learning experiences, rather than something to be avoided. Low risk-takers and perfectionists will often do anything to avoid making mistakes. Your ability to accept their well-meaning efforts in any area of endeavour, irrespective of the results, will go a long way towards determining their attitude to mistakes.

Don't get me wrong. I am not suggesting we don't praise or recognise fine performances. We simply need to practise some restraint. Just as a child who gorges himself on lollies will soon lose interest in something that was once a treat, a child who is praised for every little deed will eventually need a veritable phrasebook of positives to motivate him or her to do anything.

Praise appropriately used is a fabulous parenting tool. Let's find out how to praise.

4. Praise with impact

Praise certainly has its place, but parents need to use it in smart ways, rather than flippantly, insincerely or excessively.

Some children, particularly boys, feel awkward receiving praise unless it is given tactfully. Boys like to blend in with the crowd. They can feel very self-conscious when they are singled out in front of their siblings or peers. So praise, like criticism, is better received when given in private, or it can be misconstrued as being manipulative and not genuine, particularly when it is simply a throwaway line.

There are three types of praise that have a positive impact on children's (as well as adults') behaviour and self-esteem:

Descriptive praise. Throw a spotlight on the behaviours that kids do well. Rather than a trite 'well done', draw a word picture of what they did well and let them know its impact. Tell them what you see and how you feel. 'Wow. You have tidied really well and put everything back where it should be. It looks much better than before.' Such a comment, genuinely made, is more likely to be stored away in a child's memory and drawn on at a later date.

Summary praise. Give your children a positive label to live up to by summing up their positive behaviours with one word. 'You really worked hard to finish your project. That's what I call persistence.' 'You cleaned up the kitchen without being told. You are a self-starter.' Persistence and self-starter become part of your children's internal character reference system. Summary praise is great for kids under the age of ten as they still use their parents as reference points. Through the teenage years, peer influence has a stronger impact on self-esteem levels.

Self-praise. There are plenty of people in your child's life who are critical of them – including their peers and maybe siblings. It is a parent's job to tell kids what is right about them, so spend a little time telling your children what you see and how you feel when they do something well. Make up positive labels that they can add to their internal character reference systems and encourage them to brag a little when they have done something well. 'I did that well.' 'I'm really pleased with the way I did that.' 'I did the best I could.' 'I love the art I did at school today.' Teaching kids to self-praise can be a little tricky, but you can start by asking them how they feel about their efforts.

When you use descriptive feedback, you actually show kids how to self-praise. Self-praise is great to use with children who always want parental reassurance or approval.

Some kids need to be cued to self-praise. 'Are you pleased with yourself because you tried your best in the game?' Encourage them to say they are pleased with themselves rather than just agree with you. This gets them in the habit of self-praise.

The stage to do all these wonderful things as parents is before your children reach their teens. With kids today growing up at the speed of light this can be really challenging . . .

5. Don't pressure them to grow up too fast

As a baby boomer who grew up in the 1960s in a middle-class suburb as the youngest child of a happy family, I had an idyllic childhood. There was plenty of food on the table, lots of affection at home and heaps of attention given to the baby of a medium-sized brood. I had the freedom to visit friends, go to the shops and simply go out and play. I had a free-range childhood that few children can enjoy today.

I treasured that freedom and didn't jeopardise it by behaving poorly and risking my mother's wrath. She always found out if I messed up in public. I grew up believing that mothers know everything!

Certainly my childhood was filled with fewer adult-initiated activities such as sport and after-school lessons than my own children experienced. I had to keep myself amused and rely on my own initiative to resolve some of my problems. There were certain issues, such as friendship challenges, that I just wouldn't bother my parents with.

It is easy to get misty-eyed about the good old days. I also know that back then I sunbaked without sunscreen, I sat in the front seat of my dad's car without wearing a seatbelt and played sport without basic safety equipment. We have come a long way in a short time in these vital health and safety areas.

But my childhood was uncomplicated and allowed me to be a kid. I'm not sure the average urban childhood is quite so simple these days. Many kids today seem to me to live an adult's definition of a childhood. The period of life between the ages of three and ten is known as latency, and is a time of great learning. It is astonishing to think about the huge number of skills and knowledge that kids acquire in this period, particularly at school.

During latency kids learn about themselves. They go on a type of treasure hunt and work out what they can do and how they fit in to their many groups. It is a time of self-esteem-building. Traditionally, a long latency sets up kids for the rigours and demands of adolescence, when they try to work out who they are separate from their parents.

In latency, kids should be able to do their self-learning free from the demands of 'boy germs' and 'girl germs'; free from having to conform to the images and distractions that adolescence tends to elicit. So we need to be careful that they aren't exposed to concepts and images that drag them into adolescence before they are physically and psychologically ready.

In 2006 Clive Hamilton of the Australia Institute gave the advertising industry a pasting for its sexual exploitation of girls. Hamilton described the sexualisation of girlhood in the media as 'corporate paedophilia' and likened it to a form of child abuse.

There is no doubt that girls are dressing and acting older than ever before. They move from toys to boys in the blink of an eye. It seems that for most girls ten is the new fifteen when it comes to how they look and what they wear.

Girls have always enjoyed dressing up in their mother's clothes, but they used to put them back in their mother's wardrobes afterwards. Now many girls are wearing adult-like clothes all the time and have adult-like accessories such as mobiles and MP3 players. Nearly 50 per cent of children's parties have some part outsourced to a professional, so it seems that even their parties are adult-like.

It is hard to hide sexual imagery and adult concepts from kids. However, there are some things we can do to help our children enjoy their childhoods free from the pressure to grow up too soon. Here are three ways you can help children preserve their childhoods:

- Make sure they dress like kids and not teenagers. Padded bras for four-year-olds are out!
- Throw child-like birthday parties, resisting the temptation to hold celebrations that are too sophisticated.
- Discuss the appropriateness of images on billboards with older children, and challenge their views if they think

they are acceptable. 'This may be okay when you are older, but not now' is something that pre-teens and early teens should hear from their parents.

It takes strong, confident parenting to erect barriers around childhood and resist pester power. It also helps if a child's peer groups want to enjoy their childhoods, rather than act as mini-adults.

Now let's look at the impact peers can have on a child's development.

6. Positive peers make a huge difference

There is little doubt that positive peer relations impact on a child's academic success, their emotional well-being and state of mind. It's undeniable that we tend to reflect the views and attitudes of our peer groups. It is hugely beneficial if a child's predominant peer group cares for him, has positive expectations about the future and places high value on helping others as well as on personal improvement.

Children's peer groupings can be quite complex and dynamic. Most children will have a prime peer group consisting of between two and up to five others. These children are generally referred to as best friends, buddies or best mates. These social relationships are often formed early in children's lives and are strengthened by shared school, extracurricular or informal outside-school activities.

Children also have one or two secondary peer groups, which can be larger and generally reflect shared interests or shared best friends. When these groups contain children from different grades and even different schools, they have an insulating effect on adverse events within the primary peer group.

Being a member of a positive peer group lessens the likelihood of a child being bullied or harassed. Children in positive peer groups look out for each other and don't engage in such behaviour, whether verbal or physical. Positive peer groups tend to be tolerant of differences and loyal and caring. Having friends who care also lessens the impact of bullying and helps prevent it from impacting on other areas of a child's life.

There are a number of broad strategies parents can use to encourage positive peer groups to form and emerge. These include:

- Providing opportunities for children to mix and share experiences
- Drawing children's attention to friendship behaviours
- Focusing on socialisation rather than achievement when kids play sport or are involved in creative or group activities.

In this achievement-oriented society, we need to value positive peer relationships and ensure that they are not ignored or undervalued in our efforts to provide the best possible start for our children.

To help your child become a member of positive peer groups, try the following four ideas:

- **Discuss** with your child how a good friend behaves. Ask him to identify some buddies and talk about what makes them 'good friends'.
- Encourage him to **join** at least one outside school group and be a member of at least one school artistic, sporting or interest group.

- **Limit** your child's time in passive, solitary activities such as television viewing, computer activities and internet chat rooms.
- Make an effort to get to **know** some of your children's friends and their parents. This not only models friendly behaviours but will help you assess their appropriateness, and perhaps allay any fears you may have regarding their choice of friends.

7. Ramp up their social skills

Popularity should not be confused with sociability. A number of studies in recent decades have shown that appearance, personality type and ability impact on a child's popularity at school.

Good-looking, easygoing, talented kids usually win peer popularity polls, but that doesn't necessarily guarantee they will have friends. The children and young people who develop strong friendships have a definite set of skills that help make them easy to like, easy to relate to and easy to play with.

Friendships skills are generally developmental. That is, kids grow into these skills given exposure to different situations and with adult help.

In past generations, exposure to different situations meant opportunities to play with each other, with siblings and with older and younger friends. Children were reminded by parents about how they should act around others. They were also 'taught' from a very young age. Today's children grow up with fewer siblings, fewer opportunities for unstructured play and less freedom to explore friendships than children of even ten years ago. A parenting style that promotes a high sense of individual entitlement rather than the importance of fitting in appears to be popular at the moment. These factors can lead to delayed or arrested development in these essential friendship skills, resulting in unhappy, self-centred children.

Kids are quite egocentric and need to develop a sense of 'other' so they can successfully negotiate the many social situations that they find themselves in. As parents we often focus on the development of children's academic skills, and can quite easily neglect the development of these vitally important social skills, which contribute so much to children's happiness and well-being.

As a parent there are three ways you can help children develop friendship skills:

Immersion. Set up the environment at home so that kids learn these skills. For example, if you want your child to learn to be a good winner and loser, spend time playing a variety of age-appropriate games. Also, make sure kids have plenty of social interactions with a variety of people, including adults, in a variety of settings, both at home and outside home.

Conscious modelling. Make sure the social behaviour that you want your child to develop is on display from parents and other admired adults. So, if you want your child to develop tolerance, make sure you are friendly and complimentary to a range of people, acknowledging their quirks and frailties. Young children take their cues from you, so model tolerance if this is what you want them to learn.

Explicit teaching. Teach your child specific skills in a number of ways, including rehearsing behaviours and language, talking through specific situations as they arrive (teachable moments) and cueing specific skills (for example, remind your son or daughter to say thank you before they visit Grandma's at Christmas).

Anecdotally, it would seem that kids start school these days in better academic shape, but with a poorer set of social skills than past generations. I think we underestimate the importance of social competency to kids' well-being and, indirectly, their success at school.

Here are eight important social skills every child should have:

The ability to ask for what they want

Help children ask for what they want. It means they don't throw tantrums, whinge, sulk or expect parents to guess what's on their minds. When children are young, parents can help them to find the words they need to express themselves. We become experts after a while at interpreting what toddlers say, repeating their words back to them. We carry this on into childhood and adolescence, interpreting the silences of young people, or second-guessing grunts and shrugs. While we need to be patient with toddlers, we also need to give older children the opportunity to ask for what they want. Sometimes we need to ignore shrugs and grunts and expect our children to articulate their wishes. This is the basis of civil behaviour, as well as a basic human skill.

Good manners

Teach kids good manners, in particular the three 'power words'. These words have a way of breaking down barriers and people's defences. They can be found in every language as they have such a powerful place in human relations, regardless of the culture. These three words are: your name; please; thanks. These terms are the basis of good manners, and, when used, will increase the likelihood of getting what you want.

The ability to share possessions and space

Sharing is a basic social skill. Developmentally, very young children like to keep their possessions to themselves. As they get older and move into preschool and beyond, sharing becomes a prerequisite for playing with and forming relationships with others. Children are encouraged to play with and be with those who share their time, possessions and space. Sharing is the start of empathy, as it shows sensitivity to other people's feelings.

The ability to hold a conversation

Holding conversations with others is a lifetime friendship skill. Conversations require self-disclosure, which can be challenging for some children. Good conversationalists give of themselves, but also take an interest in the person they are talking to. Many children forget that good conversations are two-way events, and focus solely on themselves.

Within conversations, children need to learn to ask interesting questions; to take turns when speaking;

and to show they are listening by making eye contact and not interrupting.

The ability to win and lose well

Playing games requires an ability to win and lose well. Put another way, kids need to learn to win without rubbing others' noses in it, and to lose gracefully without throwing tantrums and making excuses. Wanting to win is natural, but kids must learn to do so in a way that ensures they maintain their relationship with the other players. Losing may make kids feel bad, but they must control their negative feelings so that others will play with them again.

The ability to give and receive compliments

The ability to give and receive compliments is linked to a child's self-esteem. When kids feel good about themselves, they are more likely to notice and draw attention to the deeds of others; they are also more likely to accept compliments from others. Nevertheless, regardless of esteem levels, giving and receiving compliments are skills that kids can learn. There are wrong and right ways to go about both.

The ability to approach and join a group

There are many situations throughout life where you need to start conversations with people you don't know. The ability to approach strangers in social situations opens up many doors, both friendship- and business-wise. These skills can be learned and practised during childhood so they become second nature in adulthood.

The ability to handle fights and disagreements

Disagreements happen in families and among friends. The key is to make sure they don't lead to the breakdown of friendships. It's important to get across to kids that having an argument or disagreement doesn't mean a friendship is over. Strong friendships, like strong family relationships, withstand disagreements. In fact, they often serve to strengthen friendships.

In most arguments, both parties think they are right. This is the nature of disputes. Emotions run high and things can be said that are not meant and are regretted later. Sometimes arguments are solved immediately, but often they can only be sorted out after everyone has calmed down.

8. Overcome the curse of perfectionism

Many children are afflicted by the curse of perfectionism. Firstborns in particular are prone to it. The burden of being in the parental spotlight means that many firstborns will only participate in areas where they are certain of success. So they tend to be less innovative and adventurous than later-born children.

Perfectionists can be hard to live with. They make demanding partners and anxious children. They can be critical of those around them, just as they are highly critical of themselves. Their attention to detail can be infuriating and their inflexibility enraging. Much worse, being a slave to perfectionism means kids become observers rather than participants in many aspects of life.

You can pick a perfectionist from 1000 metres away because they share common attributes. Here are nine attributes perfectionists share:

Perfectionists plan everything. They won't go on a family picnic unless the route is known beforehand, the estimated time of arrival is decided upon and the weather is checked days before. Perfectionists like to be in control, so they don't leave things to chance.

Perfectionists are neurotic about order. Tidy desks, shoes neatly arranged in wardrobes and neatly stacked food shelves are de rigueur for perfectionists.

Perfectionists are critical of themselves and others. If a perfectionist paints a room, he will focus on the inevitable thin spot rather than celebrate a job very well done. Consequently, they don't enjoy success.

Perfectionists hate to leave jobs half done. They will stay at work until a task is completed.

Perfectionists procrastinate. Many perfectionists put off starting projects because they doubt they can do them perfectly. Procrastination is not just a great stalling tactic, it is a protective strategy. They wait until conditions are perfect to start a job. The trouble is, the time is never perfect, so they never start.

Perfectionists don't like to delegate. No one, but no one, can do a job as well as they can, so they tend to take on far too much, not trusting anyone to do anything for them.

Perfectionists apologise a lot. They will always apologise that there is not enough time or money to do the job they would like to do. Perfectionists always believe that they can do better or try harder.

Perfectionists don't expect success. They are generally pessimistic and look for reasons not to do things rather than reasons to try things. Their expectations become self-fulfilling prophecies.

Perfectionists are governed by absolutes. They see the world as black and white and have strong opinions about what people should and should not do.

The best way to help perfectionists loosen up, lighten up and take risks is to develop what the great American psychologist Rudolf Dreikurs dubbed 'the courage to be imperfect'. Dreikurs maintained that we must accept our faults and avoid putting pressure on ourselves to be superhuman or better than others. When we focus all our efforts on making a contribution, rather than being better or superior, we are not held back by the need to do the perfect job.

Kids develop the courage to take risks and fail when they are less focused on themselves and more concerned about others. Perfectionists need to lower the bar they set for themselves and be realistic about what they can achieve. When they focus on others and develop more realistic expectations, not only do they end up achieving more, but they experience more fulfilment and contentment.

9. Foster volunteering in kids

'Does your child do anything to help others?' This is a question that elicits uneasy looks in my parenting seminars, but it's a valid one. Helping others is the basis of civil society. As a concept, it never really goes away; it just becomes a little unfashionable from time to time.

The first place for a child to provide service is, of course, in the family home. It is usually within his family that he first experiences the chance to help others. Opportunities are created every day for a child to show his worth to others. A child does so when he helps his younger sister get dressed or when he helps his mum or dad prepare a meal. He shows his worth when he cleans the living room, even though it may not have been his mess.

Helping others gives children the opportunity to belong in their family through contribution. Austrian psychologist Alfred Adler called such a contribution 'social interest'. Adler believed that 'social interest' was a basis for good mental health. He believed that parents and teachers should foster social interest in children from an early age by giving them tasks that help them to contribute to the whole family or a greater group. As well as teaching the skills to be independent, Adler stressed that parents and teachers need to teach children the skills to be useful to others. Adler believed that social interest is not an inborn trait; it is a trait that must be consciously developed.

Social interest fosters a sense of connectedness to others, so it enhances resilience. Heightened social interest is also linked to lower stress levels in kids and young people, as they are focused on assisting others rather than on how well they themselves perform. A number of studies link children's social interest to an increased ability to cope with life's stresses, and the pressures and demands of school. Conversely, children who are preoccupied with themselves and their performance, rather than their contribution to a group, are more likely to be perfectionists and to fear failure, as its consequences have a greater personal impact.

In many ways, the development of a sense of community is the cornerstone to mental health for children and adults. According to Adler, if children can learn social cooperation and community feeling, they are more likely to stay mentally healthy throughout life.

While volunteering begins at home, it is by no means confined to the family. Children as young as three years old can be trained to do simple household jobs that help another family member. Children in upper primary school and secondary school should be encouraged to look beyond their family for opportunities to contribute to the well-being of others. Whether it's helping a neighbour, giving up time to work behind the scenes of a school play, or becoming involved in a social-service project such as helping the homeless, volunteering not only gives kids opportunities to develop a diverse range of skills, but it helps them to develop a sense that they are recognised for their contribution or what they do, rather than who they are.

Fifteen-year-old Jessica got a huge confidence-boost from volunteering. As a young girl she seemed to lack personal confidence. She passed most subjects at school but not without a struggle. She came from a sporty family, yet she wasn't a natural when it came to ball sports, whereas her two siblings shone in those areas. She always lived in the shadow of more successful siblings. Volunteering changed that.

Jessica lived by the water, so she took up sailing at her local yacht club in her early teens. She found she was good at it, and spent most weekends during summer racing or practising. At the urging of the yacht club commodore she took a coaching course and became an instructor. She spent a lot of her spare time teaching younger kids how to sail. She enjoyed teaching and, importantly, she loved the fact that she had found something she was good at it, which she could share with others. Her experience as a volunteer instructor gave Jessica enormous self-confidence, which she couldn't get in any other area of her life at that time.

Chapter 5

Build the skills of optimism

Introduction

Optimism is not about seeing the glass as half full, as is commonly believed. Optimism relates to your belief system, about how successful you think your actions are and how effectively you feel you can make an impact on the world.

Optimists do better academically, socially and have better health than pessimists, so it makes sense to promote the skills of optimistic thinking to children. Optimists look at the flip side of negative events for some good, some hope and reason to be positive. The basis for optimism is the way a person thinks about the causes of events, which is reflected in the way he or she explains events.

As we've seen, recent American research indicates that children learn optimism or pessimism from their experiences of success and through their interactions with parents, teachers and other significant adults, as indicated by Seligman's findings. Parents and teachers model an optimistic or pessimistic attitude by the way they react to adverse and positive events in their lives.

Optimists explain adverse events in the following ways:

- **Adverse events are temporary.** 'It takes time to find a friend,' rather than 'No one likes me.'
- **Situations or causes are specific, not global.** 'I am not so good at soccer,' rather than 'I am hopeless at sport.'
- **Blame is rationalised rather than personalised.** 'I was grounded because I hit my sister,' rather than 'I was grounded because I am a bad kid.'

Pessimists have a tendency to build mountains out of molehills and give up before trying. The trouble with pessimism is that it tends to be a self-fulfilling prophecy. 'I told you I wouldn't get a kick in the game. What was the point of me even turning up?' Such comments reinforce feelings of hopelessness, which lead to a sense of helplessness.

Adults can help children and young people become optimistic thinkers with modelling and by directly teaching and drawing kids' attention to the skills of optimistic thinking.

1. Change your self-talk

Self-talk can be your greatest ally or your worst enemy. You can talk yourself up or, just as easily, talk yourself down. You can talk yourself into doing wonderful things, attempting fabulous goals. In fact, you can talk yourself into all sorts of accomplishments. You can just as easily talk yourself out of trying new activities, or assume that anything new you try will be a failure. You can succumb to the voice that says 'No,' just as you can be spurred on by the voice that says, 'YES, you can do this!'

Self-talk by itself achieves nothing. You can talk yourself up all you like, but you won't achieve anything until you take some action. However, most action, whether it moves you towards a goal or something positive, or away from a goal, is preceded by some type of self-talk. Most of us are unaware of that little voice that chatters incessantly in our heads, directing our daily activities in much the same way as a traffic cop directs traffic on a busy intersection, sending some cars through while holding up others. Our self-talk works just like the traffic cop. Sometimes our good intentions are held up by our negative self-talk, and before long we get nowhere.

Confident, optimistic kids give themselves messages in line with their abilities. Low-confidence kids and pessimists talk themselves out of doing things. Negative self-talk becomes a self-fulfilling prophecy. For example, a child who is asked to star in the school play would probably be nervous and apprehensive. His nerves are natural and in many ways helpful as they will cause him to focus, which is likely to lift his performance. But his self-talk is critical to his chances of success. A pessimist will respond, 'This is really hard and I'll probably stuff it up.' This will more than likely become a self-fulfilling prophecy. On the other hand an optimist will say, 'This is pretty challenging, but I should do okay.' If he does make some mistakes, it won't be the end of the world and he or she will more than likely try again next time. Kids' self-talk determines their attitude and how they approach any activity.

Introduce children to the notion of self-talk. Get them to listen to the little voice in their head that says they can or can't do things. An easy way to do this is to ask kids to stand in front of a mirror and listen to the voice that speaks to them. Or encourage them to write out positive messages that help them to think more confidently about risk-taking, so that the messages are reinforced. In this way, they can change the voice in their head, using alternative, realistic statements as replacements. They can repeat these statements before they approach a situation that causes them anxiety.

Parents can help kids choose realistic yet positive thought processes. This chapter will give you some ideas to help kids change their self-talk from self-defeating to more useful, realistic appraisals of themselves and the situations they face.

2. Slow down their thinking

Many children jump to conclusions when negative situations occur, so they think and act impulsively rather than checking out possible causes of events. These automatic responses may be justified if they are in line with past events, but in reality often that is not the case.

For example, a boy is walking through the schoolyard and he's hit in the face by a football. He immediately assumes someone is trying to hurt him. This is more likely if he has been on the receiving end of some rough treatment in the past. But if he stops and thinks about it, the most likely scenario is that it was merely a ball kicked by some kids involved in a game.

Similarly, a child who waits outside a shop for his friends who are ten minutes late may jump to the wrong conclusions. She could easily catastrophise and think they have schemed against her, that they tricked her into going to the shops and they were never going to meet her. They just wanted to make a fool of her. The whole situation was a set-up.

Pessimistic thinking involves this type of quick escalation into the realms of the unlikely, which can leave you feeling physically and emotionally exhausted. If this girl were to slow down and consider the options, she'd soon see there were a number of more likely scenarios, such as, they missed a bus; they were held up; no one had a watch; or they are notoriously unreliable anyway.

Parents should model this type of realistic, positive thinking out loud, so kids see how it's done. If you are the type of parent who builds a mountain out of a molehill in no time, learn to slow down and talk through the likely positive possibilities with your kids. This can be challenging as modern media has a propensity to focus on worst-case scenarios, normalising the notion of catastrophising. Media grabs and headlines frequently feature language such as, 'The worst recession in years', 'Record drought figures', 'Polls spell resounding defeat for the government'. The propensity for highlighting the worst-case rather than more likely, but less dramatic, scenarios teaches us to do the same.

The good news is we can all change our thinking. One great skill that kids can learn, which helps them to think realistically is . . .

3. Promote positive tracking

I've done a lot of work with elected student leaders and I've found that they have a predictable set of characteristics and qualities in common, including competence, trustworthiness, the ability to make and maintain friendships, and a number of other pro-social skills. Interestingly, one characteristic most share is the notion of positive tracking. That is, they look for the bright side of life and the good in others far more than they look for the negative.

Positive tracking is a wonderful life skill that any child can attain. Positive trackers tend to notice and acknowledge the good things that happen to them, rather than to focus on the one or two bad things that have happened during a day. They will walk into a room full of strangers and notice the friendly faces rather than blank faces. A positive tracker looks for the good comments in a child's school report before they find the less flattering aspects.

Positive trackers have their antennae tuned in and constantly looking for:

- Things that go well for them
- Their own and other people's strong points
- The good in negative situations
- Other people's successes
- The ability to reframe a negative into a positive

Not surprisingly, positive trackers are popular as they make others feel good. They are also more confident and appear more confident.

One practical thing parents can do to help kids positively track is to teach them the skill of reframing. That is, to develop the art of finding something positive in even the most difficult situations.

Start by getting kids to notice the good in themselves and others. Then encourage them to find something good in a bad experience:

The positive spin-off. 'It may have been a boring party, but you did meet a new friend.'

The lesson. 'You may have been unsuccessful this time, but you know what to do next time.'

The lesson about yourself. 'Maybe football, rather than cricket, is more your bag.'

The avoidance of something more unpleasant. 'You may have wrecked your skateboard, but at least you didn't get hurt.'

Positive tracking is a highly attractive quality, which elicits good fortune, well-adjusted people and even achievement. It is something that can be taught and caught.

Now I'm going to explain a fantastic way of helping kids with negative attitudes to look for the good in even the worst-case scenarios.

4. Count their blessings daily

Many children expect bad things to happen to them. Their thinking defaults to pessimism. And sometimes, like a self-fulfilling prophecy, their efforts match their expectations and they find it hard to achieve, succeed, or overcome difficulties.

American psychologist Martin Seligman explained a great way to change one's default mechanism from pessimistic to optimistic. He encourages kids to look for and count their blessings on a daily basis. You can develop this skill in a month, with some insistence and persistence.

Here's what to do. Give your child an exercise book with at least thirty-one pages – one for each day of the month. At the end of every day, children should list three good things that have happened to them during the day. Good things are defined as anything that they should be grateful or thankful for – at school, at home or outside home. Encourage them to think about some of the less significant interactions they had during the day. Negative trackers are so used to noticing bad interactions that they can miss the positive ones, such as the help of others, or someone going out of their way to include them in an activity, or listening to them when they had a problem.

This activity trains a child to look for positives rather than always be on the lookout for the negative or the worst aspect of an event. It's a very effective exercise for parents to use with their kids.

Another great way to help kids become more optimistic is to teach them the skill of positive attribution. I prefer to give it a more colloquial description . . .

5. Apportion blame correctly

Does your child take too much responsibility when something good or bad happens to him? Perhaps his sports team wins and your child, who played a great game, takes all the credit for the win. He forgets that he had some help from his teammates and coach, or that the ground suited his abilities.

Okay, we don't want to spoil the party for kids when they have something to celebrate. But it's good to introduce some balance to the picture, because kids who apportion to their actions all the good things that happen to them are set for a fall when failure, rejection and disappointment inevitably come their way. If you are prepared to be the champ, you also must accept being a chump, as life has a way of levelling itself out.

On the flip side, some kids who take all the glory take no responsibility for the bad, denying a failure they had some part in. So a child who takes all the credit when his team wins may take all the blame when his team loses, or blame everyone but himself for letting the team down. In reality, the reason for the loss lies somewhere between the two extremes.

Teach kids to attribute fairly the reasons for good and bad events and experiences that happen to them. It helps if your child understands that negative situations generally occur as a result of a mixture of three factors:

- **Me.** How much of my behaviour contributed to the situation?
- **Others.** How much did the behaviour of others contribute to the situation?
- **Luck/circumstances.** How much did luck, circumstances, unpredictable factors, such as weather, timing, lack of knowledge and illness contribute to the situation?

When your child over-blames himself or puts himself down, challenge his unrealistic statement. A child who misses a shot at goal in a football game, which would have won the game for his team, may attribute the loss of the match to his poor shot. But, given some time and space to think clearly and rationally about the situation, he should realise that others also missed shots at goal. He should acknowledge the conditions the game was played in, which made scoring difficult, and that his missed shot was only a minor contribution to the loss, as plenty of other mistakes were made throughout the game.

It all sounds logical in the cold light of day. It's a lot harder when emotion is high, so parents need to choose their time to introduce some logic to a situation. But with good parental guidance, kids can learn to apportion realistically the good and the bad that happen to them, which is a great life skill to learn. There are many times in life when one is tempted to shoulder too much responsibility for events. Those with the ability to apportion blame and responsibility commensurate to its ability have a huge advantage in terms of maintaining their mental health compared to those who take too much credit or too much blame when things go wrong.

Next, we'll look at another way to help kids who exaggerate the good and bad things that happen to them.

6. Wind back their language

Today's kids talk in extremes – 'awesome', 'the best' and 'gross' roll off their tongues easily. Extreme language leads to extreme thinking. So encourage kids to replace 'I'm furious' with 'I'm annoyed'; 'It's a disaster' with 'It's a pain'; 'I can't stand it' with 'I don't like it.' It sounds minor, but by changing your kids' language you change how they think about events and, more importantly, how they feel.

The media can take a little blame here. Next time you watch a reality program aimed at young people, check out the language used in the show. It is always full of absolutes. Everything is black or white – 'the best ever' or 'the worst ever'. 'Superstar' or 'super dud'. There are no shades of grey. Exaggeration rules! Moderation is boring.

So what's my point? People who talk in absolutes ('I'm furious' rather than 'I'm annoyed') or imperative terms ('I must do it' rather than 'I'll try to do it') often get stuck in inflexible, unrealistic thinking and behaviour patterns. And they bring a lot of stress upon themselves. People who are more flexible in their thinking and approach to life tend to have better mental health and are more successful.

So, the next time you feel annoyed about a situation, ensure your response is not out of proportion to the event, and if it may be, tone down your language. You'll instantly start to feel better and more in control. This is a great coping skill, I can assure you.

The same holds true for children and young people. When they ramp up a situation with over-the-top language, let them know that they can turn the catastrophe switch down a few notches. Something bad that happens to them may just be a 'pain in the 'neck' rather than 'the worst thing ever'; 'disappointing' rather than 'devastating'.

Kids will often switch you off if you don't appear to be listening on an emotional level, or if you always seem to disagree with what they say. So you need to be careful how you respond when dealing with catastrophisers and exaggerators, particularly when your kids are upset. Here are a couple of techniques I've found useful:

> **Reflective listening, but winding it back.** Acknowledge your child's issue, but gradually wind back their thinking by suggesting different terms: 'Yes, I can see how you probably can't stand it. I wouldn't like it either'; 'I can see how you think it's the worst thing to ever happen to you. Yes, it would be unpleasant, but I'm sure it will improve.'

> **Suggestive questioning.** Question kids' reactions and gently suggest some different responses. 'Was it really devastating, or was it disappointing so you feel let down?'

7. Handling anxiety in kids

For those with no personal experience of anxiety, it can be hard to understand how debilitating it can be. 'Come on, get on with it,' seems the obvious solution. Of course, this response is nowhere near adequate.

Around one in ten children struggle with anxiety. Nearly 50 per cent of adult sufferers say it began in childhood. Presumably they weren't taught the skills to cope as kids so their anxiety became entrenched as they grew older.

Most kids, like adults, experience some anxious moments or have fearful thoughts and feelings from time to time about certain events. These thoughts and feelings prompt them to proceed with caution rather than to rush in where angels fear to tread.

But anxiety and fear can be paralysing. Some kids simply can't stop their 'bad thoughts and feelings'. They can't silence the voice of fear that continually whispers to them.

Parents are an obvious choice to help their children overcome anxious moments. Remember, anxiety is a normal part of life and can be managed, but it takes time and it can't be solved in one conversation. Anxiety is contagious. Parents and children can feed each other's anxieties. So it's the job of parents to stay calm, think clearly and role-model confidence when kids get anxious.

Calm is created through your words, voice and facial expression. When children become anxious, help them to recognise what is happening. Some kids get angry, some become upset and others withdraw. Work out the pattern for your child and help them to recognise when they are anxious.

Accept your child's feelings. Your child needs to trust that you are with them, then they will be more willing to let you help them cope. It can be difficult at times to differentiate between what is a bad case of negative thinking and true anxiety, which needs attention and assistance. Is a child being negative when she doesn't want to join a new club because she thinks no one will like her, or is there something more going on? Try your best to confirm whether there is any validity in her fears. If not, diplomatically point out she may be catastrophising. If you feel she has foundation for her concern, she will need support to overcome her anxiety.

Challenge the validity of your child's fears and anxiety using logic and rational thinking. Don't allow kids to wallow in self-pity. Move their thoughts towards the future rather than allow them to mope around.

Encourage your child to overcome their anxiety through action. One mother came up with a creative solution to help her seven-year-old daughter, Ruth, get over her reluctance to attend her schoolmates' birthday parties without her mother. Being a good mum, she attended parties with her daughter so she wouldn't miss out on these social opportunities. But her daughter was becoming too reliant on her so it was time to make a change.

The next time Ruth was invited to a party, her mum put a plan into action. First, she set up a little birthday-party scenario at home using dolls and teddies as friends, so her daughter would know what to expect when she went to the party. Ruth's mum explained that she would leave her at the party for a short time on her own, while she did some shopping. She let her daughter know that she would have a terrific time and that she had no doubt she'd cope.

The little plan worked a treat. Vanessa arrived at the party an hour after it began to find Ruth busily involved in a game. She acknowledged her mum but she didn't leave the game. Later, at home, Vanessa made a fuss over her daughter for being brave and overcoming her fears. Ruth agreed that next time she was invited to a party she would go for the whole time without her mum.

Now we'll look at kids who wear their hearts on their sleeves and are easily hurt by others' remarks.

8. Raising sensitive souls

Do you have a sensitive child? You know – a child who takes every-thing you or others say to heart; a child who has a thin skin and worries too much, particularly about things out of their control. Sensitive kids worry about what others think of them. They often sense danger well before others and see the consequences of behaviours well before their peers.

Is such sensitivity nature or nurture? I suspect the former is the culprit. It has been estimated that 15 per cent of children are born with a more sensitive temperament – that is, a temperament that makes them particularly aware of their surroundings and of any changes that may occur.

Sensitive kids are like mood detectives, with their antennae up trying to detect subtle changes in the moods of those around them. In some ways this is healthy, as emotionally intelligent people are tuned into the behaviour and feelings of others. Sensitive kids generally have high emotional intelligence quotients.

However, typically sensitive kids often read too much into what others say or do. Sometimes parents will say something without thinking, or a friend will ignore them for a whole day for no other reason than that they were being self-absorbed. Sensitive kids take these matters to heart. They take the mistakes of others and turn them into something they are not. They see a simple blunder as a personal slight or something sinister. Sensitive kids can think too much and read too much into simple situations. That's why they can become anxious, shy or both. They can be hard to live with.

If you have a sensitive child, you need to see and appreciate both their sides. The side we most often see is the shy, inhibited, fearful worrier. The flip side is that sensitive kids generally have kind hearts, are empathetic, intuitive and usually possess a creative streak. These are wonderful attributes to have.

As the world kids inhabit at school is akin to a jungle, sensitive souls are open to being hurt by their peers. Kids who wear their heart on their sleeve and who have a timid side that is fairly visible can sometimes be given a harder time by their more confident, resilient peers, just as those who look and act a little differently from the norm are susceptible to teasing and the like.

Research over the past decade into the area of children's sensitivity and anxiety by Professor Paula Barrett from the University of Queensland revealed that 40 per cent of sensitive kids experience some form of real anxiety. The secret of the 60 per cent of kids who don't experience anxiety is certain 'protective' factors. The top of this list is parenting style. Sensitive kids benefit from having an optimistic, resilient parent who supports them, but doesn't allow them to take themselves too seriously. It also helps if parents can encourage their child to take risks socially and applaud their successes, no matter how minor. It is good if parents are supportive; even better if a parent is resilient so that the sensitive child sees how to cope with some of life's hurts, rejections and disappointments. In fact, sensitive kids are less likely to develop anxiety if at least one parent is 'thick-skinned', positive, even jovial. Kids need a parent who gets across the message that there are some unpleasant events in life, but we can learn to cope with them and the world is generally a great place.

When sensitive kids are raised in a balanced way with proper understanding and encouragement, they are well-placed to grow up to be happy, healthy, well-adjusted and creative adults.

Section 3

Developing character in kids

Character is an old-fashioned term. I recall references to it on my primary-school report cards. The teachers rated my character, making comments about my behaviour in support of the marks they had given me. Character went out of fashion for a time, but it is now making something of a renaissance. You read and hear a great deal about it these days. Sports teams are said to show character when they win against the odds, politicians are supported when they demonstrate good character and pilloried if their behaviour drops below certain standards. Individuals display strength of character when they overcome odds to succeed in any field of endeavour, whether as adventurers, in the arts or in business.

Character means many things, but it usually refers to a set of personal traits or qualities that help one to succeed and achieve. Any list of positive character traits will be long, but would include qualities such as persistence, courage, humility, generosity, self-regulation, curiosity and resourcefulness.

Hear someone say, 'That person showed real character' and you know it's more than mere personality that is being referred to. Character in this context refers to moral strength, reliability and the ability to hang in there.

To my mind, the development of good character in kids should be a primary goal for parents. We all have our own definition of character that reflects our background, experiences and values. From my perspective, developing character in kids is about promoting behaviours and attitudes that maximise their chances for individual success, but at the same time ensures their social success. It is also about promoting a set of strong personal values to act as a type of moral compass, assisting kids to choose behaviour that keeps them safe, maintain the rights of others and makes a contribution to the groups of which they are part.

Kids with a strong sense of identity and character have healthy attitudes towards themselves and others. They:

1. Persist in the face of hardships.
2. Give rather than take from the groups they are in. They volunteer to help – not for praise or to receive accolades, but because they know it's the right thing to do.
3. Practise impulse control. They put off immediate gratification so they can reach a longer-term goal.
4. Have a strong sense of social conscience that's shown through their reliability, honesty and ability to keep personal confidences.
5. Empathise with others, particularly those less fortunate than them.
6. Have a strong sense of right and wrong and are not easily dissuaded from these core beliefs.
7. Are loyal to the people and groups that they value. They will stick up for these people when necessary.

In the next two chapters I will focus on how you can promote a strong sense of character in your kids. The focus will be on influencing children's behaviour so that they fit into their family and other groups. We must also teach kids to develop respectful attitudes towards others, as well as to develop a strong sense of right and wrong based on the universal values of tolerance, mutual respect, personal responsibility, cooperation and the right to be safe and feel protected.

Chapter 6

Get kids behaving well

Introduction

The last few decades have seen dramatic shifts in styles of discipline, which reflect widespread social changes. In countries such as the United States, the United Kingdom and Australia, the approach to discipline has swung between a very child-centric approach, when it seemed parents had forgotten that they were the adults in the relationship, to the current use of parent-focused techniques that place control firmly back in their hands. The use of praise and a reliance on reward systems to promote appropriate behaviour are the hallmarks of the child-centred approaches.

Despite the variety of approaches available, parents still struggle to get discipline right. Recent Australian research shows that 58 per cent of parents struggle to find an appropriate approach to disciplining their children. Anecdotal evidence suggests that American parents have similar dilemmas. Parents today want to use different discipline techniques from their parents, yet they are unsure which to use. In Australia, parents rate the development of positive attachments and good relationships with their children as their highest priority. This desire to maintain strong relationships means that many are reluctant to discipline their children – they have an understandable desire to be the good guy because they feel this is the only way to maintain a positive relationship with their children. However, many parents forget that even 'good guys' can have a mean streak now and then.

While society has changed significantly over the last few decades, children and their developmental needs haven't altered much. Children develop best in a stable environment where they are valued, loved and listened to. They prefer an orderly environment rather than a chaotic one. And they need someone in that environment who will help them to learn to be safe and sociable, which is what discipline is about.

Children in the first few years of life are hard work for any parent. Parents today are poorly prepared compared to their predecessors for just how big a challenge children of this age can be. Their comparative lack of exposure to children prior to parenthood, compared to past generations', means that many are flabbergasted when confronted with developmentally normal misbehaviours that many two-year-olds display. This age group experiences massive physical development that is not matched by the same rate of intellectual maturation. Children around the age of eighteen to thirty months are like international airports – a massive amount of activity is governed by very small control towers. Children in the two-to-three-year age group generally present the most challenges to parents behaviourally, with the eleven-to-fourteen-year age group a close second. It is not surprising that these two ages present most difficulty, as both are significant transition stages, during which the pursuit of independence is paramount.

Kids need discipline. They always have and always will. They don't respond well to the rigid approaches that many parents used in the past, but that doesn't mean they are now in charge. It's sometimes hard knowing what approach to use. However, there's plenty of evidence to show that well-adjusted children have parents who create supportive environments where the rules and boundaries are clear and adult behaviour is consistent. Firmness and consistency are associated with independence, provided the control doesn't excessively restrict a child's wish to be spontaneous or to experiment.

Effective discipline is balanced between control and freedom;

between a child's wish to experiment and his need to conform; and between the need to make demands on others and his ability to respond to the demands that others make on him. It uses behavioural consequences to teach appropriate behaviour, and recognises that adult approval is a powerful driver for most kids.

In this section we'll look at some tools and techniques to teach your kids to behave well and to be able to fit into the different groups in their lives.

1. Get more cooperation

Obedience. Remember that term. 'Obey your elders' was something many of us as kids were constantly told. The concept of obedience belongs to a bygone era when kids were seen and not heard and respect was hierarchical rather than mutual. Obedience has been replaced by the concept of 'cooperation', which takes more skill and effort to attain.

How to get kids to cooperate is perhaps the biggest challenge for many parents. Cooperation is dependent on goodwill between parents and their offspring. Kids can withhold their cooperation if they believe you are not acting in their best interests. They have a built-in radar that will detect when you take short cuts with them.

You can build a spirit of cooperation so that 'helping out' and 'doing the right thing' become part of your family culture. You need to model cooperative behaviours and expect kids to cooperate with you. Expectations are a powerful tool for parents. You get what you expect, so expect kids to help out!

Cooperation is usually invited or won. You can invite kids to cooperate, but you can't demand that they do. (Of course, when a child's safety is paramount, you may need to insist they comply with your demands in order to keep them safe.) Your language plays a part in persuading your child to work together with you. 'Grandma's coming to visit. What can we do to make her stay enjoyable?' is more effective in eliciting cooperation than telling your child he or she must make her feel welcome. Kids are more likely to stick to decisions they have had a say in.

Families that develop a spirit of cooperation usually have three distinct values that drive their behaviour. These are independence, shared responsibility and mutual respect. Kids grow away in a physical sense from their parents. Independence means that they develop a set of skills and attitudes that enable them to operate independently. Shared responsibility means that the family does not depend on one person, rather everyone has an impact. Mutual respect means that we treat each other with respect, and we insist that kids treat us in respectful ways. These values drive our behaviour and our treatment of each other in our families.

Parents who elicit cooperation use a distinct set of strategies consistently, which promote family involvement and responsible behaviour. Here are three, very different strategies that promote cooperation in families:

> **Recognition.** Make sure you recognise when kids are being cooperative. Give them feedback, which describes what they have done and how it affected you: 'It was great the way you came to the table the first time I asked. It makes my life easier.' Parental recognition is a big influence on most kids, regardless of age.

Language of cooperation. Parents who use the language of coercion or control rarely get lasting cooperation. The language of coercion is littered with directives, demands and commands. Nothing wrong with telling kids to do something from time to time, but if you are always demanding and commanding, some will just tune out, and some will learn to fight you all the time. The language of cooperation involves asking for help, using choices and stating problems so that your children can step up to the plate because it's the right thing to do, rather than because it's demanded.

Family meetings. This is the big cooperative family strategy I discussed earlier. It takes some effort and some learning to put into practice. But when you use this strategy well, you will find that you are more able to develop a sense of 'we' rather than 'me' within your family.

It would be great to think that cooperation happens easily in families and kids naturally want to help and please you. But this is faulty thinking, as groups by their nature need effective leadership to make them gel. Families are tricky groups to lead, so it takes some pretty effective leadership to get kids singing from your songbook.

Therefore, the parenting strategies you use make all the difference when it comes to getting cooperation from kids. Consistency is essential, so read on . . .

2. Consistency is the key

Evidence suggests that parents of young children need to adopt an approach to discipline that is heavy on teaching rather than the punitive stuff. My own work with generation-X-led families suggests that parents who base their discipline on the principle of consistency generally raise well-behaved kids and enjoy positive relationships with them, which is nirvana for all parents, regardless of their generation!

Parental consistency gives children a sense of security and control. Consistency means parents deal effectively with little mis-behaviours so they do not grow into bigger ones. It means parents follow through and ensure children experience a consequence when they misbehave. It also means that both parents in a dual-parent relationship have a similar approach to behaviour. Children learn from a young age to play off one parent against each other when their standards differ.

Consistency, like routine, is often sacrificed by busy parents and put in the 'too-hard basket'. When parents are tired, stretched and overworked the last thing they want to do is engage in a battle with children over what are sometimes petty issues. Besides, consistency can make a well-meaning parent who values relationships feel downright awful. But giving in rather than holding ground is not a smart long-term strategy. Kids learn quickly how far they can push a parent before they give in. If parents give in occasionally children will learn that if they push hard enough and long enough they will eventually win. Consistency is about being strong. Consistent parents do the following:

Say what they mean and mean what they say. Knowing the difference between a threat and a warning is important for parents of children of all ages. 'If you keep messing around we will cancel our next holiday' is the type of threat that few generation Z kids would fall for. 'Throw toys one more time in this store and we go home immediately' is a well-timed warning that can be followed through.

Don't allow moods to dictate your response to children's misbehaviour. Sometimes we are lenient when we're in a good mood, but come down hard on the same behaviour because we've had a bad day and our mood is awful. As hard as it seems, we need to be immune to our moods when we discipline. Sticking to known rules helps you take the emotion out the equation, so as much as possible be guided by the notion of family rules and common-sense limits to teach kids to behave.

Do not cave in when children push the boundaries. When children ask for a treat and parents say no, they need to keep saying no, no matter how persistent the child is.

Confer with the other parent if possible. When both parents give a child the same message and show similar resolve over issues, they send the message that they are working together.

3. Make it easy for kids to behave well

Getting kids to behave well is a dilemma for many parents. Discipline is thought to be reactive – that is, it is something we do after kids have behaved poorly. But it is also about being proactive – in other words making it is easy for kids to behave well. Most kids want to behave well, but some find it difficult. So it helps if parents make it as easy as possible for their children to do the right thing.

Three tools that will help them to behave well are cueing, grooming and shaping. Here's how each works:

> **Cueing.** Sometimes kids need to be cued into the behaviour you want. This means you give them some warning, time to cooperate and a reminder. For instance, you may give a toddler a few warnings about what is coming next. 'You're going to have a story soon.' 'Story time in a minute!' 'Story time now!' You may prompt them to behave well. 'It's bedtime. What's the first thing you need to do now?' Cueing is best used when you know you are breaking into whatever children are doing and there may be some resistance, or when children need a hand to remember what to do.

> **Training.** This refers to training kids in certain ways so they are prepared for future situations. It is about forming effective habits that become second nature. For instance, you groom kids to use manners in public by expecting them to use manners with you. You train kids to be independent when they are young so that doing things for themselves becomes second nature when they

go to school. They think nothing of making their own snacks because they have always done it.

Shaping. There are many ways to shape behaviour, but the best is describing kids being good, or mirroring. Describe kids behaving well so that they get an understanding about their behaviour and its positive effects on others. For instance, you might describe how you want them to greet a stranger or behave in a new situation. 'When we go round to see Ella, she'd like it if you said a nice hello to her.' Alternatively, or additionally, you can give an accurate description after they have behaved well. 'That was clever, the way you looked Ella in the eye and said her name when you said hello.'

I am sure parents of the past cued, groomed and shaped the behaviour they wanted in their children. They just didn't use those names. Never mind what the tools are called. Quite simply, the more time you spend making it easy for kids to behave well, the less time you spend correcting poor behaviour, and the better kids will feel about themselves.

Limit-setting is also an important parenting tool . . .

4. Set expandable limits that teach

Limits and boundaries make kids feel secure and allow for healthy development. They are simple ground rules that teach children how to behave and how to be safe and social.

Parents these days can be unsure about setting reasonable

160

limits and boundaries. But they are an essential part of discipline – the foundation for positive, cooperative behaviour.

Boys, in particular, learn through their use. Put boys in a group situation and they like to know what the rules are and who's in charge. Both genders love to push against them – it's their job! The average child will push against parental boundaries with tantrums, whining and arguing about 30 per cent of the time. More difficult children will do so twice as much. So you need a backbone and thick skin when you implement limits and boundaries, particularly with some toddlers, teens and argumentative types.

When they are used well, they are super-effective. Recently, I saw a neighbour teaching his four-year-old son about safe riding. The little boy was told he could ride his bike on the footpath for two blocks in either direction from his house. The limits the father set worked well because they were clear, specific and realistic. Clear, because the boy had the two-house limit explained to him in language he understood. Specific, because two houses is immediately measurable for the boy and he knows the difference between the footpath and the road. Realistic, because the instructions were within the four-year-old's skill and experience range. They made sense to him. The limits weren't fuzzy ('Ride carefully'), general ('Don't go too far') or unrealistic ('You can't ride outside').

This type of limit-setting can be applied to any situation and age group, including teenagers. 'You can go out tonight, but I expect you home by eleven o'clock' is the attitude here. Of course, the limits depend on your kids' ages and the situation involved.

A smart management technique with teenagers is to involve them in the limit-setting process. I'm not suggesting that everything should be negotiated, but in my experience teens are more likely to stick to boundaries under such circumstances. There are no guarantees though.

One smart way to extend limits is by rewarding responsible behaviour with greater freedom. The four-year-old may have his riding range extended when he shows he can ride safely in the restricted area. If your teenage daughter has consistently made it back before her curfew for some time, perhaps it's time to agree to extend it a little bit.

5. Avoid your first impulse when kids misbehave

Think back to the last time one of your children behaved poorly. How did you react? Did you yell, whine or roll your eyes?

Whatever your reaction, my guess is that you probably acted impulsively, without thinking. Of course, as a parent you get tired, stressed and frustrated, and children's poor or uncooperative behaviour merely makes you more tired, stressed and frustrated. So the cycle continues.

The trouble with impulsive parental reactions to children's misbehaviour is that they usually encourage the behaviour rather than diminish it. Ever said to your child something like, 'If I've told you once I've told you a thousand times, don't . . .'

If you have, there is a good chance that this statement simply fed the behaviour that was annoying you. The reason is that most misbehaviour that involves you as a parent is purposeful. It is not a conscious decision, but there is a pay-off for the child. Let's face it, most parents are as predictable as washing-machine cycles when kids misbehave.

So next time your child whines, argues or refuses to go to bed, avoid your first impulse. Don't tell them to stop whining. Avoid getting involved in arguments of their making. Resist reminding your child to get to bed (he or she already heard you the first time). Change your first response, which is to focus on them. Instead, focus on yourself and your behaviour:

> **Stay calm.** Think about what's behind their reaction and act accordingly. If the behaviour is about getting your attention, then direct your attention elsewhere. If it's about getting their own way, refuse to fight.

> **Act, rather than speak.** Allow natural or logical consequences to do their magic. Put the meal on the table and let it get cold rather than remind your children yet again to come. Then take it away after ten minutes. Consequences get you out of the picture. Consequences stop you from arguing or staying involved with a child's behavioural issue. Consequences, when delivered calmly and reasonably, put the onus back on the child to change. The key is not to be fussed about a child's choice. If he chooses to go hungry for a night rather than come to the table, so be it.

The key when kids don't cooperate is to talk less and act more. And that's hard to do if you react impulsively when they misbehave.

6. More action and fewer words cure parent-deafness

Ever asked your child for help and been underwhelmed by the response? If so, did you repeat your request, as most of us would? Still ignored? Then my bet is you tweaked up the volume until you got a reaction.

If this sounds familiar, your children have a bad dose of parent-deafness, a common affliction. If you want to check, try whispering, 'Anyone for ice cream?' A few minutes later ask for help. I can bet the responses will be very different! The good news is, there is a cure for parent-deaf kids. But first it's important to understand how your child caught parent-deafness in the first place.

Parents tend to respond quite predictably when their children don't cooperate. The four common mistakes that lead to parent-deafness are:

Repeating requests and reminders. Most kids know how often Mum and Dad will repeat themselves before they act. They know it may take Mum four times but Dad will go ballistic if they ignore him. They pretty much understand their parents' typical reactions by the age of four.

Turning up the volume. Some kids will only respond to a raised voice because only then do they decide their parents mean what they say.

Using coercive language. Most kids at some stage like to have their own way. They respond better to choices and reasonable requests rather than demands because then they feel in control. This can be challenging for bossy or controlling parents.

Delivering a lecture. Kids' eyes glaze over when their parents move into lecture mode.

These methods of communication happen when parents are tired and stressed, but they are largely ineffective.

So what is the cure for parent-deafness?

When you want kids to cooperate rather than ignore you, first make sure you've got their attention. The best way to do so is to move closer and make eye contact. Then be brief with your instructions. Simply ask for help, remind them it's time for bed or let them know dinner is being served.

If you get no reaction, avoid repeating yourself or raising your voice. Keep those well-meaning lectures about how kids should help for another time and put a consequence into place. That means you stop what you are doing if they don't help, or start reading the bedtime story in their bedroom even if they are dawdling. Or, as I mentioned before, you put their meal on the table and take it away if they are still not there when you've finished yours.

The point to remember is that kids learn from your behaviour, not your words, at this point. Your willingness to act in a reasonable, respectful way is the key here. Most of us talk too much to our kids when we want cooperation, which trains them to tune out rather than to take notice.

Most kids like to please their parents, so it's worth making a fuss when they have done the right thing. Catching them doing the right thing means they are more likely to do it again. No guarantees, mind you! Just likelihoods!

Sometimes the tone of your voice rather than your choice of words get the cooperation you require. Find out more . . .

7. Talk to kids like a composer, so they listen

Listen to yourself talk to your children. Take note of the words you choose and, more importantly, the tone of your voice. Does your tone match your words?

Children tune into tone as much as words. Toddlers learn from the tone of your voice whether you are pleased or mad at them. The words matter little as their vocabularies are developing, but the tone of your voice, which matches the look on your face, conveys the message.

Children will often ignore words if they are not matched by your tone of voice. 'Put your toys away, please, and come to the table,' is a simple instruction that can be said a number of ways. If your tone is whiney, you are indicating that you don't expect your child to comply. You are teaching your child to ignore you. If your tone is aggressive, you are issuing a challenge to disobey, which some kids can't resist. If your tone is friendly yet firm, your chances of getting cooperation will increase dramatically: your expectation is being conveyed respectfully and happily.

Tone of voice is an indicator of mood and kids are natural mood detectives. It is a useful skill that prepares them for preschool, school and life beyond. However, if their home environment is chaotic or dangerous, all their energy is taken up checking the moods of the adults in their lives, which is not in their best interests. These children are often highly stressed and anxious.

Communication between parents and kids is like a song – made up of lyrics and music. A good composer attends to both the lyrics and the tune, making sure they match.

Kids will attend to the melody (tone) of your voice rather than the lyrics (words). Most of us focus on the lyrics rather than the melody when we speak to our kids. Get a mismatch and we either teach our kids to tune out or we confuse them, and they may wonder what is wrong with us or them.

Think like a composer next time you have something important to say to your children, or you simply want to make sure you're getting through to them – i.e. focus on the melody as much as the lyrics. Get the match right and your communication will be far more effective. Here's another idea that helps . . .

8. Use the proximity principle to be heard

The proximity principle is a deceptively powerful little concept. I learned about it as I observed teachers and parents managing the communications and behaviour of children over a period. The good operators, I noted, were conscious when dealing with children of the time, place and space they worked in, particularly with kids who were upset or angry.

If you want your children to really hear you, you need to move into their proximal space. That is different to invading their personal space. A child's proximal space is the space about an arm's length away from them. Move closer and you are invading their personal space which, for many, 'sends them off' as they feel threatened.

You also need to consider the timing of your communication. As a general rule, avoid talking with kids when either of you are angry. You also need to be mindful of where communication occurs. For instance, kids are more receptive to messages when you are both seated, as this is the 'conversation' position. Also, speaking in private is more effective than in public.

The proximity principle is a simple idea but it has a wide application. Let's look at some examples.

- A mother at the beach is yelling at her five-year-old to stop throwing sand. At ten metres away from her child she has little joy. She then moves into her son's proximal space (about a metre away), which means she lowers her voice and makes eye contact. The result is her son stops throwing sand and changes activities.

- A teenager comes home from school and is greeted with 'How was your day?' from her high-energy dad. Her response is an uninterested shrug. Dad changes tack and waits until his daughter is sitting near him until he begins another conversation. This time he makes a connection and she is far more receptive.

- A ten-year-old throws a tantrum in the supermarket as his mother won't buy a certain item. His mother avoids getting into conflict here. She just grins and bears it – but she doesn't give in. Later, at home, she sits down near him when he is relaxed and revisits the situation. He is more open to listening to her as she has made good use of the proximity principle of time, place and space.

The proximity principle is blindingly obvious. However, due to many factors, we often neglect to use it. I know when my communication falls on deaf ears it's usually because I have neglected some aspect of the proximity principle. Now I'm letting you in on some of my real secrets! Practise it and you'll wonder why you didn't put it to good use before.

9. Use choices to get cooperation

Anyone with decent communication skills and a backbone can get easy kids to cooperate. Getting cooperation from the children and teenagers who dawdle, argue or just plain dig in their heels when they're asked to do something can be a huge challenge.

You need to know what you are doing when you handle these kids or else parenting becomes one big battle. As we've seen, use the language of coercion ('Do this and do it now!') with them, as many adults do, and all you'll get is resistance.

These kids love to feel they are in control, so you need to use language that doesn't threaten them. That's why using choices can be so powerful in gaining their cooperation – the kids think they are calling the shots, but it's an illusion of power because in fact you control the choices.

To be effective with choices you need to follow these steps:

- Give these kids a choice of two things only.
- Give them a choice of what they can do: 'If you want to play roughly, please go outside. If you want to stay inside, you need to be quiet.'
- If this fails, cue them: 'You can go outside on your own steam, or I'll take you outside.' Tough nuts often choose the path of least resistance!
- Speak in a non-emotive manner, as if the path they choose has no bearing on you.

10. Use consequences to change behaviour

Smacking, corporal punishment and other less savoury means of getting cooperation from kids, such as shouting at them, are currently out of favour, but the use of consequences is in. I love the notion of behavioural consequences. They are the best way of teaching children to take greater responsibility for their lives and to make smarter choices. Parents can use two types of consequences – natural and logical consequences.

A logical consequence is used most frequently in family situations. It requires adult intervention and is used when a child's behaviour disturbs other people. A child who makes a noise in the family room is asked to leave; children who fight in the family room lose the right to watch television there; and children who refuse to clean their toys lose them for a period of time.

Effective logical consequences are related to children's misdemeanours, and are reasonable and respectful of their dignity. For example: a toddler starts chucking water out of his bath so he is removed quickly. A brother and sister start fighting in a shopping mall so they are bundled into the car and taken home. A young girl leaves her doll in the garden after being told to bring it inside, only to discover her mother has confiscated it.

A natural consequence involves no adult interference. For instance, a child who leaves a raincoat at home will get wet; a child who spends all his pocket money on Monday will have nothing for the weekend; and a child who oversleeps and misses the bus walks to school. In these examples children learn from the direct consequences of their own decisions or actions, and thus they are not protected from negative outcomes from their parents.

But do note that you should not use natural consequences when safety is an issue or when children are too young to understand the outcomes they will elicit.

Here are some tips for using consequences effectively:

Allow yourself some time for consideration before setting a consequence. Judges are smart. They find you guilty one day and bring you back for sentencing on another. They separate the emotion of the trial from the objectivity of sentencing. If you issue consequences in the heat of the moment, you may end up asking the impossible and have to rescind it.

Consider giving probation for first offences. Be forgiving of first offences and consider giving a warning before issuing your consequence. Kids will consider compassion a strength, not a weakness.

Avoid life sentences. Judges are loath to bring down life sentences, which give no hope or incentive for improved behaviour. Ban a teen from going out for a two weeks rather than leaving the duration open-ended. Set a timeframe for the consequences and be reasonable.

Don't acquiesce to terrorism. If your child issues a threat such as, 'There is no way you can make me come home at six o'clock,' don't rise to the bait. Deflect it by saying, 'We'll talk about this tomorrow.' Don't give in to threats of running away or non-cooperation: 'I hope you don't run away. It's great having you at home. I want what is best for you.' Avoid stating what you'd love to say, which maybe something like, 'Yeah, try running away. You wouldn't last inside two days before you were back begging for a good feed and a comfortable bed!'

11. Develop impulse control

Between 1968 and 1974, Stanford University researcher Michael Mischel conducted an unusual experiment that demonstrated the importance to one's lifelong success of delaying gratification.

In a long-term study, Mischel offered four-year-olds a marshmallow and told them that if they could wait for the experimenter to return after twenty minutes, he would reward their patience with another marshmallow. Control your impulses and delay gratification for a greater reward was the idea here. An interesting dilemma for any forty-four-year-old, let alone a four-year old.

Mischel found the results divided the kids into three groups. About one-third ate the marshmallow within the first few seconds. They didn't even consider waiting. Down the hatch! Another third tried to wait, but couldn't last the distance. Another third practised some old-fashioned self-discipline and didn't eat the marshmallow. That's quite an effort!

Mischel followed the 400 kids involved in the experiment over a fourteen-year period and found that there was a high correlation between the results of the study and how each group performed in high school.

The marshmallow gobblers had difficulty subordinating their immediate impulses to achieve long-term goals and were more troubled adults. When it came to study, they were easily distracted and less likely to finish school.

The marshmallow resisters were more motivated, educationally more successful and more emotionally intelligent. Their end-of-high-school marks were higher than the other groups'.

Sometimes we can draw too many conclusions from such experiments. In fact, a study such as this one can take on a life of its own, and be quoted out of context without any real understanding of how it was conducted.

But this study seems to prove beyond question that impulse control is one of the keys to achieving highly in life. Nor does it take a study to make that obvious. Those who can put off immediate gratification or the quick fix to work towards a bigger goal will always be successful. It takes self-discipline to save, rather than use a credit card. It takes self-discipline to get up in the cold each morning to exercise rather than stay in bed. Impulse control pays off . . . in the long run.

Modern parenting can be detrimental to developing impulse control. Let's face it, in this era of smaller families, we have a greater propensity to gratify our kids' desires immediately. I see some adults bending over backwards to give their kids what they want to avoid disappointing them.

Impulse control is largely about self-discipline and character. While some kids are more naturally prone to delay gratification than others, some parenting styles are more likely to promote impulse control than others. Parenting does have an impact!

Here are four strategies to encourage your children to delay gratification, practise self-discipline and build character along the way:

Just say NO! You may need to gird your loins when dealing with tough nuts, but so be it.

Give kids pocket money and teach them how to set goals. Being a child's personal ATM doesn't encourage impulse control.

Help kids focus on bigger rewards. When kids can see that a bigger reward is attainable, they are more likely strive to get it.

Establish rituals and rites of passage. 'You get your big bike when you're ten' is a type of ritual that parents used in the past to make children wait. These rituals and rites of passage give parents the strength to resist pester power and teach kids that good things come to those who wait.

12. When you lose your temper

Ever blown your top in front of your children, only to regret it ten minutes later? Silly question – it happens to us all, no matter how well-behaved our kids, or how placid and patient we are. At times the strains and stresses of life wear us down, so our emotional responses don't match our children's behaviour. Or rather, their less-than-perfect behaviour doesn't warrant the 'screaming banshee' response that you have provided.

So what do you do if you have blown your top and given your children an absolute verbal blast, as steam pours out of both your ears?

First, check that your rare outburst of anger is just that – rare. I don't want to state the bleeding obvious, but constant sudden outbursts of anger are a sign that all is not right with you. Perhaps you need to take a break, get some additional help with your kids or even get some professional counselling to sort out any internal or relationship issues you have.

If your outburst is rare, the best response is to apologise. Put a little time between your outburst and your apology and consider giving an explanation: 'Sorry about yelling at you guys. I have been working so hard lately. I guess I need a break.' No need to grovel, just reveal your human side to your family. Your children will take their cues from you and if they see you reveal your vulnerability, it gives them permission to reveal theirs.

It is a good idea to check your anger levels from time to time. When you know you are under stress and feel you're about to blow your top, take a break, phone someone (and vent your annoyance on them, if possible), or simply count to twenty (or one hundred) to help to control yourself in front of your kids.

However, there is a place for parent anger in the discipline process – as long as it is controlled. There are the times when children really need to know they have crossed a line and your whole voice and attitude needs to convey that their behaviour is unacceptable.

Most parents will know the type of response I am referring to. Your voice goes steely and the words come out purposefully. Eye contact is strong and body language is direct. The kids aren't frightened. They just know that that their mum or dad means what they say. Gulp!

This type of response should be saved for times when your children are putting each other down mercilessly, and won't stop doing so when asked, or when they have shown gross disrespect to themselves, others or their environment.

We all want to steer clear of angry responses when we interact with those we love. But being human means that our behaviour doesn't always reach the lofty heights we would like it to, and at times we lose our cool.

So, recognise the signs of pending anger and take steps to

manage it, and if you do lose the plot, reveal your vulnerability and apologise. Nothing wrong with that!

13. You can say no to teens!

Two mums came to me, fretting over a decision they had to make. Their daughters, both of whom had just turned thirteen, had asked for permission to go out on a Saturday-night party bus with over forty sixteen- and seventeen-year-olds.

A party bus is a nightclub on wheels for young people. There is supervision and the buses are promoted as alcohol-free, but they can be badly supervised and sleazy. The mums knew little about this one.

The two girls put huge pressure on their mothers to let them go – pester power was alive and well in their homes in the days preceding the planned night out. It was the first time their mothers had been put on the spot in such a way, so they sought my advice. Both admitted to me that alarm bells were ringing and they didn't feel good about letting their daughters go on the bus.

My response was simple and straightforward: 'You *can* say no!'

The main issues were the age gap between the girls and the rest of the party, and the mothers' lack of knowledge about who was attending and the exact nature of supervision on the bus. Both girls were in the early stages of adolescence, when they considered themselves to be several years older than they actually were.

The emergent teen desperately wants to act 'older' and be older than he or she actually is. And kids in the early stages of adolescence draw strength from each other and rarely make parental challenges individually, or at least not without some back-up.

'Everyone else is going,' 'Bonnie's mum is letting her go,' are the catchcries for this age group, as they battle to break down resistance from their parents. That's why they gang up on parents. Not only is it more effective, but working together gives them false bravado.

Many young teens think they have invented adolescence, but they have no idea what they don't know. They can't see, or won't see, potential risks involved in things they want to do. Parents need to be the 'bad guy' for this age group, making decisions for them in their best interests.

So what did the mums decide?

Despite their gut instincts, and my advice, both of them let their kids join the Saturday-night party bus. Fortunately, their kids showed more common-sense than their parents! The young teens didn't like what they saw when they were dropped off to start the evening. They didn't feel safe, so they returned home with their parents.

There are three salient lessons from this scenario.

First, it was evident that these mothers didn't feel confident enough to assert their authority over their daughters. They were confused about how they should respond, yet their gut instinct was giving them a strong message. Next time, they should have more faith in their instincts.

Second, like many parents, they were working in isolation. Although they were good friends, it wasn't until the morning of the party that they spoke to each other. By this time their daughters' pestering had worked a treat. Next time they should call for second, third and fourth opinions.

Third, as both these girls were the eldest in their families, their parents were unaware of the developmental stages of adolescence and the approach needed at each stage. It was their first real experience of the teenage push for independence. They were flying blind, and this is not a good way to raise teens.

So would you fret over this decision? Would it make you sweat? How prepared are you to face a similar dilemma? As a parent of teens, I know that situations like this happen out of the blue. Confidence in your approach is probably the best ally you have. Confidence in your authority gives you the backbone to walk away from arguments and resist pestering. The confidence gained by understanding what each stage of adolescence needs helps you make clear decisions in your children's best interest, at an age when they most need good, firm parenting.

The key to raising teens is to be prepared, and many parents are woefully unprepared for the challenges they will face at this stage in their kids' lives. There is nothing like experience, but it helps to have an understanding about teen development, a knowledge of the best approach to raising teens, a number of allies and friends with whom you can swap ideas and, importantly, from whom you can draw strength when your resolve and patience are put to the test.

And of course, you can just say NO!

Chapter 7

Dealing with tough nuts and tricky situations

Introduction

Discipline is easy when you have easy kids, but a lot more difficult when they are challenging. This section will look at ways to manage the behaviour of more challenging children and handle some of the trickier situations that many parents face.

1. Raising high-maintenance kids

'I would have stopped at one child if my second child had been born first,' said a mother at a recent parenting seminar. Can you relate to this sentiment?

Nature has a way of evening out the score for parents. If you have an easy firstborn, hang on to your hat because the chances are you will have a later born who will require more of your time and energy. In other words, you will have a high-maintenance child.

High-maintenance kids are demanding, exasperating and exhausting. They can be tearful, self-indulgent, argumentative, bossy and just plain stubborn.

High-maintenance kids always want more – more possessions, more of your attention and more of your time. They never have enough of these commodities. Spend all day with such a child and they wonder why you won't spend the night with them too. High-maintenance kids can be like jack-in-the-boxes at bedtime. Put them to bed and they emerge ten minutes later wanting a drink, a kiss or one more book. But what they really want is YOU!

They also take you away from your other children. You would love to spend more time with Perfect Pete, but Turbo Terry, Argumentative Aaron or Whining Wilhelmina keep on at you so that Pete never gets a look-in.

There is no magic pill if you have a high-maintenance child.

Yes, some children are diagnosed with ADHD (Attention Deficit Hyperactivity Disorder) and given medication in the form of Ritalin. These little pills have become very popular over the last decade as the number of children diagnosed with ADHD has increased dramatically. Only recently have we as a community begun to question the wisdom of giving this drug to young people.

Most high-maintenance children don't fall into the ADHD category. They are simply extreme attention-seekers who need to be weaned off their parents' B-grade or negative attention. We become so adept at responding to these kids' misbehaviours that giving them an enormous amount of attention becomes habitual. If you are the type of parent who likes to be helpful, you'll be at the beck and call of such kids all day.

One solution is to stop giving them attention when they misbehave. When they want your attention, do something completely different. Ignore the whining and it will increase in volume. Ignore a child's constant interruptions while you are on the telephone and be prepared for an ear-splitting shriek or even a mess. The bad behaviour will generally get worse before it gets better – that is the norm with high-maintenance children, and why they are such hard work. But it's useful to change your own reactions to your child's behaviour, so he or she doesn't get the satisfaction of getting a rise out of you.

Here are some other strategies for reducing the impact of high-maintenance kids:

> **Make yourself scarce.** Although it's worth trying, it is hard to ignore high-maintenance kids, so another strategy is to keep yourself busy, or make yourself scarce.

This can force them to draw on their own resources. Just be prepared to give them plenty of attention when you are around.

Do the unexpected. Sometimes acting from left field is your best ally when you have kids who make constant demands on your time. If you have a child who continually whinges, invite him to sit down and listen to you have a good old whine about your day. 'You've had a bad day, you should hear about mine . . .' He'll be off like a shot rather than listen to a whining parent.

Attend more to needs, and less to wants. Be clear in your own mind about the difference between a 'want' and a 'need'. High-maintenance kids have more wants than needs. For instance, they may want ice cream, but they don't need it. They need food. A toddler may need you to cut up his food, but he wants you to sit with him while he eats. He doesn't need you to sit with him. Understand the difference between wants and needs. Attend more to needs and less to wants.

2. Win cooperation from 'make me' kids

Ever been in a power struggle with a child that you know you can't win?

Most families have at least one child who likes to have their own way and doesn't like to be told what to do. I call them 'make me' kids because when they are being challenged, everything about their demeanour demands you 'make them' do as you want. Power struggles between parents and children are common. Often the 'make me' and the 'I will make you' battle becomes more important than the issue we are fighting or arguing over in the first place. A simple desire for control is behind many of the power struggles between parents and kids.

If you are locked in a power struggle, you will forever be battling unless you make some adjustments. Start by checking the language you use. Forget the 'Do this and do it now!' approach with these kids. It may have cut it in the past and it may be effective with 'easy' kids, but it doesn't work with kids who like to be the boss. These kids respond well to the language of cooperation, which involves choice and is more about asking for assistance than demanding help. You don't have to beg, but you do need to mind your language with these power-seekers and remember that cooperation is won, not demanded.

Here are some strategies to use that will increase the likelihood of getting cooperation from 'make me' kids who like to be the boss:

> **Don't fight over every issue.** Cut the boss some slack and
> let them make decisions themselves. If you want a say in
> every area of their lives, you'll soon find yourself locked
> in battles over relatively inconsequential issues such as
> clothing, bedroom tidiness and food. For instance, if a
> young child doesn't want to wear a jumper in winter, so
> be it. But if he won't clean his teeth in the morning or
> the evening, perhaps this is something to address. I see
> parents exhaust themselves over minor battles so that
> when big issues come up they give in!

Tell them what you will do. Most of us tell kids what they should do, and they promptly ignore it. It's far better to tell them what you will do. This is a subtle shift in language, which has a huge impact in getting cooperation from 'make me' kids. Here are some examples: 'I'll serve ice creams when you're seated at the table.' 'I'll listen to you when you've calmed down.' 'I'll drive when you're quiet.' Get into the habit of focusing on what you will do, rather than on what they should do, and you'll start to get more cooperative behaviour almost immediately.

Let consequences do their magic: Of course, you need to stop reminding kids about their behaviour and allow them to experience the consequences of some of their poor choices. This removes you from the power struggle and allows experience to be their teacher.

'Make me' kids challenge parents who are naturally authoritarian, or who were raised in authoritarian ways. These kids are often referred to as stubborn, disobedient, pig-headed and argumentative. The flip side is that they can be strong-willed, assertive and determined individuals. Either way, they can present challenges to us as parents managing them on a day-to-day basis. Next I'll look at a particularly annoying behaviour that many parents face . . .

3. Don't pick up the rope!

Recently, I saw a fourteen-year-old girl taunt her mother in a way that only young adolescent girls can do. The mother was in a hurry to go to an evening meeting and asked her daughter if she could walk the family dog. It was not normally this girl's job, but it was a reasonable request, given in a reasonable way.

But her daughter wasn't going to be reasonable. She stood in the kitchen and belligerently replied, 'Why me? Why don't you ask someone else?'

This young girl threw down an imaginary rope (the last word, a taunt, a jibe, a joke) for her mother to pick up.

'Don't pick it up! Just let it go!' I thought as I waited for this mum to leave. 'Your daughter's going to walk the dog, but she's not going to do it graciously.'

But the mother did pick up the rope, giving her daughter as many reasons as she could think of why she should help: 'I drive you around the countryside from one activity to another. I do it because I love you. I ask you to do one thing and you turn it into an argument.'

I detected the slightest grin on her daughter's face that said, 'Gotcha!'

It's hard to ignore some of the verbal comments kids throw our way. I'm not suggesting that we turn a blind eye to taunts or rude remarks, but there are many occasions when we should just leave the imaginary rope a child throws where it lies because usually when we pick it up, we turn into a child too!

'Throwing down the rope' is effective because the profound issues of power, position and prestige are behind most conflict between kids and adults. And arguments or comeback lines, which are often about kids saving face, threaten our position or prestige as parents.

They are a way of kids saying, 'I will acquiesce to you, but on my terms,' which is also about power.

So next time a child 'throws the rope', look at the imaginary rope, smile and refuse to pick it up. It's the adult thing to do.

4. Disciplining kids who learn the hard way

Does your child act before he thinks? Does he pat a dog, even though you warned him not to? Does she ignore a 'wet paint, don't touch' sign and check it out for herself? If you're nodding your head, chances are your child likes to learn through trial and error.

'You can tell me all you want, but I'm going to find out for myself' is the motto of such kids. They don't like to be told. Experience is their teacher. The lessons learned at the school of hard knocks can be bitter, which makes parenting these kids pretty tough.

Inside school, these kids are hands-on and tactile. They love to experiment and tinker. They learn about flight by making paper aeroplanes and flying them through their classrooms. They'll adjust the nose, tail and wings to make their plane fly for a longer distance.

They learn about human behaviour by watching the reactions of classmates as the aeroplanes fly. They'll notice that some people will react differently. Mates will love it and most likely laugh. Others will cringe and roll their eyes.

They learn about limits when the teacher keeps them back after class for flying paper aeroplanes in the wrong place at the wrong time. They'll adjust their behaviour to avoid being kept in. But if the pay-off is big enough, in terms of getting a reaction from peers, they may choose to continue flying paper aeroplanes in class instead. The pay-off is worth the risk of being caught!

These trial-and-error kids will test the boundaries parents

set, and ignore their well-meaning advice. They are more likely to be boys and more likely to be a worry in the teenage years, which are highly experimental anyway. The risks of learning this way when young are likely to simply involve scraped knees, hurt egos and disappointment – minor compared to the risks that teens can take. These can be scary, but they don't mean parents should shelter their older kids.

I know of one parent who shielded her son from the consequences of his poor choice rather than let him learn a valuable lesson. Seventeen-year-old Jarrod went to a gathering with some of his friends one Saturday evening. His friend's big brother got them a supply of alcohol and Jarrod got drunk with his mates. He drank until he blacked out. He woke the next morning with a terrible hangover. He was still sick on Monday morning when he had to sit an exam at school that counted towards his end-of-year marks. He confessed to his mother what he had done and said he couldn't go to school that day and sit his test. His mother contacted his school, saying that her son was sick. The school agreed to allow him to sit the test another day.

This well-meaning mum protected her son from the consequences of making a poor choice, rather than letting him face up to the consequences of his actions. Her son, a classic trial-and-error kid, missed a great learning opportunity due to overprotective parenting. He is less likely to modify his behaviour and think ahead the next time he's in a similar situation if he knows he has someone who will rescue him from his poor choices.

Here are some tips for parenting trial-and-error kids so they stay safe but absorb lessons along the way:

Make their problem, their problem. Often as adults we take on our kids' concerns and make them our own. If something doesn't bother them and there is no risk or infringement to other people's rights, let them be. If they leave their school lunch at home, it shouldn't bother you.

Let them experience natural consequences. Natural consequences are fabulous teachers, so step back and allow these kids to experience the outcome of their decisions, pleasant or unpleasant. So a child who leaves his rain jacket at home will get wet and learn to think ahead next time the clouds look grey.

Save them from themselves. Differentiate between safe and unsafe risks. The use of natural consequences doesn't apply when a child's safety or well-being is at risk. The story of the mothers who had to decide whether or not to let their vulnerable daughters ride on the party bus is testament to this.

Link behaviour with outcomes. Sometimes the lessons kids should learn need some explaining. So be prepared to reinforce life's lesson if they don't seem to understand the outcome of their behaviour: 'The reason your friends don't go to the cinema with you is that you talk all the way through the film.'

Sometimes lessons take a while to sink in, so you need to be patient and repeat your explanations. It may seem like nagging but there is often no other way.

Allowing kids to absorb life's lessons is a tough gig for parents. But for some kids and some situations, it's the only option.

Another tough gig is dealing with kids' tantrums. Kids of all ages throw them, but how you deal with them will determine whether or not they continue.

5. Taming temper tantrums

Tantrums come in various guises. They can be noisy with lots of shouting. They can be quite physical, with doors slammed and objects thrown. And they can be silent, which can be just as difficult to manage as the louder kinds. Kids of all ages throw them, but the frequency is a little higher in the toddler and teenage age groups.

Kids throw two types of tantrums. The first is a frustration tantrum, when they can't do or explain things adequately. Throwing a tantrum is a way of venting that most of us grow out of. It may be valid for a four-year-old to throw his shoes in the air because he can't tie up his laces, but it's embarrassing when an adult tosses his work in the air if he has missed a deadline. But it happens! When kids throw a frustration tantrum, adults need to reassure them, give them space or even give them a hug until they have calmed down.

The other type of tantrum comes from a different space altogether: a control tantrum. These are the wobblies kids throw when things don't go their way. When they want to demonstrate their disapproval or get what they want, a tantrum magically appears. These tantrums are forms of emotional blackmail, which are very effective in helping kids get their own way. Control tantrums require an audience – the bigger the better – so supermarkets and other public places make great places for them. Children may throw a tantrum in their bedrooms, too, but always loud enough for parents to hear. They are often thrown at a particularly inopportune time, when they're hard to resist, such as when you are racing out to work in the morning.

Tantrums are very energising. Next time you are feeling lethargic, try throwing yourself on the ground and yelling and you'll soon feel the adrenalin pumping. In this way, tantrums can take on a life of their own.

So how can you respond to control tantrums so they decrease rather than increase? Here are some ideas to consider:

If possible, get on top of tantrums before they begin. As soon as you see the first sign of a 'wobbly', act quickly to prevent it from escalating. Use distraction, be firm, but don't let the tantrum take off.

When a tantrum begins, move away. Don't try to reason with a child in the middle of a tantrum. Go into another room, or even outside. If the tantrum is in public, either move away (but stay close enough for supervision) or quietly remove the child from the scene. Refuse to be around or cooperate with a tantrum-thrower.

Be firm and refuse to be blackmailed by your children's outbursts. Giving in sends a message that tantrums work. If a child makes a mess or becomes destructive, he or she must clean up the mess or make some type of restitution later, when things have calmed down. By remaining calm and refusing to give in to temper tantrums, you are sending a powerful message: 'I will not be blackmailed by such behaviour. I shall respond positively to you when you calm down.'

Following a tantrum, talk about more effective ways in which your child could act to get his or her needs met. Rehearse what they could do next time, down to what they could say. This type of rehearsal can be very effective in teaching children more appropriate ways to get attention.

Provide a safe alternative for children who want to display their anger. Exercise, hitting a ball or even quiet relaxation can help dissipate anger, if the anger is a problem. Talk about these safe alternatives with your child.

Now, if there's one behaviour that makes me want to throw a tantrum, it's when kids go to one parent to get the response they want, after the other has denied them.

6. Desperately seeking yes

Ever had a child who keeps asking for a favour or a treat until you say yes? These kids generally use one of two strategies. They either nag or hound you until they get a 'yes' out of you, or they seek out the adult who will give them the answer they want.

The first method, which is based on persistence, is generally effective with tired or single parents. 'All right, you can have an ice cream. Anything for some peace and quiet,' is a response familiar to many parents.

The second method is a little more devious, but just as effective, and occurs in many dual-parent families. A child's request for a treat, favour or outing is turned down for good reason. 'No,

Jessica, you can't have an ice cream now. It's nearly dinner time.' So your child asks your partner the same question, hoping for an affirmative response.

These situations can drive you crazy and can indicate that two parents are not communicating well enough. If it happens every now and again, it is no big deal. However, if one parent is always granting a child his or her wish without consultation with or consideration for how the other parent thinks, it is time to step back and reflect on how you can both work together.

If this type of parental manipulation occurs in your family, you and your partner need to discuss how you deal with it, and how you can communicate more effectively to block it. A child quickly becomes aware if his or her parents have different standards of behaviour. This means that parents need to discuss and settle on a 'party line', which they both adhere to consistently on relevant questions. They also need to get the message across to their child or children that it's unacceptable to seek out either Mum or Dad to get the response they want.

Parents must be alert to and firm with the child who goes to their partner in search of a yes:

'Where did you get that ice cream from? I already said no.'

'Daddy said I could have it.'

'I'm sorry, but you shouldn't go to Daddy after I've said no.'

The other technique you can use, which is very effective if one parent is a jellyfish and gives in all the time, is to defer to your partner whenever your child has a tricky request.

'Okay, Jessica, I'll just check with Dad and I'll get back to you.'

This strategy can be wearing, even artificial, but it's helpful to bring the other parent into the act and also demonstrates that you are not a solo act.

It's not just partners that have difficulty working together. Similar challenges can be presented when your friends' or relatives' children misbehave . . .

7. Disciplining other people's kids

Imagine a friend has visited and her little darlings have turned into monsters the minute they walked through your front door – climbing over your furniture, continually interrupting your conversations and being obnoxious and rude – yet your friend has done nothing about their behaviour.

Disciplining other peoples' kids is tricky these days. Despite the idealistic rhetoric of 'It takes a village to raise a child,' child-rearing nowadays is a very private activity, and parents can be protective of not only their own children but their methods of raising them. Disciplining someone else's child in public can be taken as a personal affront to the effectiveness of their parent.

Disciplining a friend or relative's child is easier if you are on the same wavelength and have similar expectations about behaviour and discipline. But it's really challenging to do so when your standards of behaviour are postcodes apart, or the other parent's idea of discipline consists of a few feeble requests for some politeness, which their kids routinely ignore.

The key is to communicate with the other parent, to be clear about who is going to do the disciplining and to reach an agreement on acceptable behaviours when you are together.

The following guidelines may help with this process:

House rules apply. If children are visiting your house, the rules of acceptable behaviour that you normally expect should apply. Don't be afraid to pull up children with an appeal to adhere to house rules, such as: 'We don't play on the furniture here. Climbing is for outside in this house.' Then enforce your rule and lead them outside if they continue to play roughly inside.

Deal with misbehaviour directed at you. Respond to children's cheeky behaviour, poor language, or lack of manners if it's directed at you or impacts on you. Kids need to learn that different people accept different standards of behaviour and they should adjust theirs accordingly.

Check with the other parent if you are unsure. If you see inappropriate behaviour, check with the child's parent about who should deal with it. Ask about their way of disciplining and agree with them about who will handle it if they won't, or don't, see the behaviour as an issue.

Keep discipline reasonable with other people's kids. Stick to behavioural consequences that are reasonable and respectful to the child. Never smack or verbally criticise another person's child, no matter how poorly they behave. This is acting outside the realm of acceptable adult behaviour. Keep your discipline in line with what is generally acceptable in child-care centres and schools and you can't go too far wrong.

Working with parents whose standards are different from yours takes some tact and diplomacy and a willingness to make a stand about behaviour you feel is unacceptable, regardless of who the parents are.

Sometimes children's behaviour can be a little unusual, to say the least . . .

8. Managing disturbing behaviour

'I'm going to hold my breath and it's your fault.'

Four-year-old Timothy had found a great way to worry the heck out of his parents and get his own way at the same time. It was bedtime and Timothy was a serial bedtime resister. Holding his breath until he turned blue was his latest trick and it worked a treat. His mum and dad would usually cave in and give him some extra time in the adult world. Anything to see him exhale!

Kids holding their breath is just one of many weird and way-out things children will do, which can be disturbing for parents. It's difficult to know how to respond to such behaviour, particularly when it appears kids are harming themselves.

As a rule of thumb, children don't *generally* harm themselves. They may threaten, they may bluff and they may even experiment a little, but they will rarely deliberately hurt themselves. If you buy the notion that kids don't act in a vacuum and that their behaviour needs a pay-off, it is easy to understand what's behind some seemingly harmful behaviours such breath-holding, vomiting and head-banging. They can be great ways to get their own way or pay back their parents for making them do something they didn't want to do.

Let's look at some common disturbing behaviours and work out some possible responses:

Head-banging. This disturbing behaviour belongs in the autism spectrum. If your child bangs his or head on a hard surface such as a cot continuously and purpose-lessly causing real harm, there may be cause for concern. Get him or her checked out professionally.

Some kids hit their heads as a type of experiment and stop when it really does hurt. Others hit their heads as part of a tantrum. It is best in these cases to calm them with a hug or a back rub.

Vomiting at will. Kids can throw such a big tantrum that they end up gagging and throwing up. Don't be too concerned if this is the case. Kids have also been known to throw up at will, particularly when their parents want them to eat certain foods or do something they don't want to.

Soiling pants. It is not uncommon for young boys to be so involved in a game that they forget to go to the toilet and end up soiling themselves. Fun is on their minds. The key here is to make sure the kids, not just the parents, are involved in the clean-up process so next time they won't be too preoccupied to go to the toilet. But make sure you don't do it in a way that embarrasses them.

Biting. This is a common behaviour among toddlers,

usually boys, who are very oral by nature. Get them to bite on a frozen orange (I kid you not) if biting persists. Otherwise, swift removal from the scene with a brief explanation as to why is your best bet.

If these disturbing behaviours are frequent and not aimed at parents, it may be wise to seek professional assistance. The key question to ask yourself is: 'Would my child behave this way if I was not around?' If the answer is yes, it may be necessary to get some help.

9. My child did *what*?

Some time ago a friend contacted me, shocked and distressed by the poor behaviour of her five-year-old child. It seems the little girl insulted a schoolmate by making unpleasant references to her weight as they lined up for school. And she did so in front of the parents of the child.

This mother felt mortified and stunned by her daughter's out-of-character behaviour. What should she do and say?

We want our kids to treat others with tolerance, respect and fairness, to accept people's differences. Not to judge a book by its cover. To remember that beauty is skin deep, but true worth goes deeper. These are the messages that every right-minded, caring parent spends considerable time and effort developing in their kids. And, most of the time, they will follow the messages and values that you promote.

But kids are kids. As every parent knows, children will often say what they are thinking. They are not constrained by the same social mechanisms as adults. These come with age – a little later for boys than girls!

Kids also have L plates when it comes to learning a range of behaviours and skills, whether they are physical or social. They spend time working out what's appropriate and what's not, which means a little boundary-testing is usual.

The school ground, just like preschools, can be something of a jungle. Away from the gaze and scrutiny of adults, kids can treat each other differently than we would like. They can be downright cruel to each other and say some awful things.

Kids do work out their own pecking orders and coping mechanisms, and they need space from adults to allow this to occur. That is not to say that we as adults should adopt a 'whatever!' approach and leave kids to themselves. As every experienced parent, teacher and carer knows, there is some behaviour you let go and some you correct. We preach and teach good messages at home, and cross our fingers and hope they stick when our kids get to school. As a former teacher I know that, by and large, kids represent their parents' and family values well at school, but not always to the degree their parents hope.

So what could this mother have done about her daughter's comment? What approach should she take? After all, this is a classic teachable moment and requires some type of positive parental response.

These were my suggestions:

Don't take her behaviour personally. Easier said than done, but we often unjustly judge our performance as parents by our children's behaviour. This is fraught with danger!

Let her daughter know that she was unimpressed with her behaviour, and put it in the context of behaving like a good friend should. In other words, is this how a good friend would act? How should a good friend act?

Revisit the comment later at home and create a little empathy. Encourage the girl to identify with her school-mate so she has an understanding of the impact her remarks might have had. How would she feel if someone called her fat, skinny or stupid?

Sometimes it's useful to get a child to apologise. This can be a little meaningless, though, if their heart is not in it. For children in middle primary school and above, it is useful if the child asks the girl or boy they offended if they will forgive them. This requires a response from the offended person and can reseal the relationship.

My last piece of advice, having revisited the comment, was to move on. I wouldn't be surprised if the offended girl already had.

Section 4
Promoting resilience

The development of resilience in children has both mental-health and learning benefits. From a mental-health perspective, kids need to develop a set of broad coping mechanisms that will enable them to manage, both emotionally and practically, some of the setbacks and hurdles they will experience every day.

There are five factors that contribute to children's and young people's resilience:

1. **Spirit.** Some kids have resilient spirits. They are born that way. You know these kids because they spring back quickly from adversity. Sometimes they can really test us with their spirited behaviour, but it's an asset when the chips are down.

   Spirit consists of many characteristics, including determination and persistence; the propensity to focus unflinchingly on a goal, the ability to laugh in the face of adversity.

2. **Skills.** Resilient kids share a number of different skills that enable them to bounce back from some of life's hardships. There are four basic skills that kids pick up from their environment, either through teaching or modelling. The broad skills of resilience are:

   Independence. The development of self-help skills and the ability to function freely and safely outside the family.

   Problem-solving. The ability to resolve many of their own problems in their own way.

Optimism. A way of thinking about the world that shows a belief in being successful and overcoming hurdles.

Social skills. Includes the ability to empathise, and a set of coping skills such the use of humour and compartmentalising, so that one negative event doesn't spoil everything else.

3. **Support.** The quality of the support kids get from adults will determine how they react to some of life's difficulties. Kids who have the assistance of at least one attentive, healthy adult are more resilient than those who are surrounded by inattentive, stressed adults. The impact of one supportive adult is immense when kids experience difficult times.

4. **Self-esteem.** Kids' sense of self is often tested by adverse events. Kids who have a positive sense of themselves built on a solid foundation of competency ('I am capable because I can do lots of things') and mirrored messages ('my mum tells me I'm clever so I must be') are less adversely affected by some of the social difficulties they may experience. Self-esteem Teflon-coats kids against criticism and social rejection.

5. **Hardships, frustration and difficulties.** Kids' previous experience of minor adversity helps them cope with major adversity. Either consciously or unconsciously they reach back and use the skills they have developed through previous experience to help get them through.

I include in this 'stuff', hardships, frustration and difficulties (HFDs).

There are six common or developmental HFDs that kids experience on a regular basis: disappointment, loss, change, rejection, conflict and failure. Sometimes parents want to protect their children from experiencing these difficulties. But it's better to help them develop ways of coping and of overcoming such difficulties.

In this section, I will focus on strategies you can use that will develop a lasting sense of resilience in your kids.

Chapter 8
Build their mental health and coping skills

Introduction

Kids typically face many HFDs as they get older. Pets pass away. Friends move. Families move and children change schools. They miss being picked for a team. They are left off party invitation lists.

How stressful these everyday events are for them will depend on many factors, including their own spirit, the support they get from home and their coping skills.

Coping with HFDs, both big and small, is part of growing up. Some kids seem to naturally get by. Others need parental support to help them cope with seemingly minor situations.

It's useful to reflect on how you manage when life throws you curveballs. Healthy adults develop a series of coping mechanisms to draw on, often instinctively, when they experience stress or some difficulty, so they don't become overwhelmed.

It helps to share your coping mechanisms with your children. It's very reassuring for kids to know that their parents also experience and overcome difficulty.

1. Help kids unwind

Modern kids are busy kids. Regardless of their age, their days are likely to be filled with activities. Under-fives might do a range of adult-initiated learning activities designed to give them the best start to their learning lives. School-aged kids have a huge range of leisure and after-school activities to choose from. It's not uncommon for kids to have four or five extra-curricular activities a week.

There's nothing wrong with kids being busy, as long as they have plenty of chances to relax and unwind. Relaxation is key to good mental health and well-being.

One way to ensure busy kids unwind is to let them get bored every so often. There is a temptation to fill each day with activities so that no time is wasted. 'I'm bored!' is the last thing most parents want to hear their kids say. Many parents feel compelled to do something to alleviate a child's boredom. But there is nothing wrong with a little boredom now and then. Boredom can be good for kids, giving them the chance to muck around and take it easy for a time.

Here are five ways to help your kids unwind:

Let your kids regularly 'stare into the fire'. Ever sat around a campfire and stared at the flames? If so, you will know how calming it is. No exertion! No need to think! No need to talk to anyone! Just a chance to chill out and relax. The TV is the modern version of the campfire. Yep, TV used in this way for school-aged children is good for their mental health; just don't let them stare at it for too long.

Let kids exercise without rules. Kids have always been the kings and queens of play until lately, when their lives have become highly organised and scheduled. Free, child-initiated play is the ultimate in relaxation. Fun games, games with few rules and games that kids control help them to unwind.

Let kids experience 'flow'. 'Flow' is a state we get into when we are so engrossed in an activity that time disappears. It is the ultimate unwind. We achieve flow when we pursue our passions, so encourage teens to find activities that they truly love and get lost in. Free play generally takes young children to 'flow' very quickly, so opportunities for unstructured play are essential.

Help kids calm down around bedtime. Have a bedtime routine that calms down kids rather than winding them up. You can become part of this routine by giving baths, reading books, telling nursery rhymes, providing soothing back rubs and using other means that work for your children.

Unwind with your kids. When I was young, the best times I had with my dad were spent in the backyard playing cricket. Sounds like a cliché, I know. It was fun because it was never a chore for him. He loved it, as it was a chance for him to unwind after work. Find ways you can unwind and rejuvenate with your kids.

We want our kids to be busy and be engaged rather than inactive and apathetic. However, activity needs to be balanced with unscheduled time so that perspective as well as everyone's sanity is maintained.

2. Keep things in perspective

It's natural when things go wrong to think that life will never be the same again. I recall as a teenager doing less well than I'd expected in my end-of-school exams, and missing the course I had chosen. At the time it was a catastrophe. I thought that there was no point taking another course as I would hate it. In the end I did a teaching course, which I really enjoyed and I didn't look back.

Breaking up with a friend, losing a sporting contest or being on the receiving end of teasing can seem like events we'll never recover from. But catastrophising only exaggerates your worries and makes you more anxious. It always helps to keep your sense of proportion, but it's not easy when emotions run high. We all catastrophise from time to time, particularly when we are under stress. It takes a cool customer to moderate their thinking the whole time, but some kids are prone to jumping to the worst-case scenario, even when a problem is quite minor. If your child is a serial catastrophiser, you can change their thinking so they learn to keep things in perspective.

Here are three ways to challenge your child's catastrophic thinking:

'What's the most likely scenario?' Sometimes it's useful to introduce a dose of old-fashioned rational thinking to kids who always think the worst will happen to them. 'Yep, you could break your leg if you go skiing. But the odds are that you won't.'

One way of dealing with catastrophisers is to admit that they could be right, but even if the worst-case scenario does happen, the sun will still shine tomorrow. Take kids to the worst-possible scenario and they may see it's not so bad after all. This is the type of reality check many kids need.

'Where does this fit on the disaster meter?' Catastrophisers get themselves in a knot about relatively insignificant things. Okay, making a fool out of themselves in front of their class may not be insignificant to many kids, but compared to plenty of other events it is fairly trivial. Perspective is a good thing. Help them get some perspective by giving their worry a score out of ten on how important the issue really is.

'That's unhelpful thinking.' Sometimes kids' thinking is so out of whack with reality that they become anxious about minor things. Thinking, 'Everyone must like me,' 'I must never make a mistake' and 'Bad things always happen to me' are extreme and need to be replaced by more moderate, realistic thoughts, such as, 'It would be nice if everyone liked me, but not everyone will,' 'I am bound to make some mistakes, but I'll survive them,' 'Like anyone, some bad things have happened to me, but lots of good things too.'

Knowing that they are not the only one to experience a hardship or recover from a difficult situation is very reassuring for kids. Sometimes they can think they are the only one to experience a difficulty . . .

3. Normalise the situation

It's human nature to think that we are the only ones to experience something bad. But the human condition dictates that this is rarely the case. Everyone has experienced loss, rejection, disappointment and conflict in their lives. Rarely is there a situation so unique that you are the only person to have experienced it. Normalising a situation is an aspect of optimism. When you realise that others have experienced similar difficulties and survived, you feel more hopeful.

When bad things happen to kids, help them to normalise

the situation rather than personalise it. Even when they experience extremely distressing events such as family breakdown, help them understand that other families break down too and, as difficult as it may seem, everyone emerges intact. It's reassuring to know that others have gone through similar situations and learned to cope.

From a mental-health perspective, we need to allow children to experience the full gamut of emotions, including sadness, loss, fear and anxiety. These emotions are normal and healthy. Kids need to hear that: 'Everyone feels bad sometimes,' 'It's okay to feel sad or scared. Most people would be in this situation,' 'You are not the first person that this has happened to.' They also need to be allowed to express their emotions. They need to have genuine worries and disappointments validated, but they also benefit from someone close to them reminding them that, 'This too will pass and life will return to normal.'

Next we'll look at some more ways to help kids cope when life gets tough.

4. Get away from it all

When life's stressful for kids, they need to take a break from situations that worry or sadden them, or cause them stress.

My mum was an expert at taking my mind off such things. When I was young, I was upset that a neighbour's dog had killed my guinea pig. My mum took me to a movie that afternoon as a treat. She knew the best way to help me to deal with this big shock was to get me out of the house for a while. The technical term for what my mum did is 'adaptive distancing'. My mum wasn't thinking in those terms. She instinctively knew that the best way to help me and stop me from brooding was to distract me for a while.

When kids are troubled by events, or spend too much time brooding, do something like my mother did: play a game, spend time together, have a treat, watch some TV, go out – do something different with your children.

One way for kids to temporarily escape their troubles is through hobbies and interests other than school and family. As I've said, the ability to lose yourself in an activity you enjoy is one of the best mental-health activities you can do. Young people who are completing end-of-year exams benefit from a circuit-breaker to freshen them up and release some of the pressure they are under.

Self-distraction is another skill to teach kids who constantly replay bad events in their minds. It prevents them from doing so and blowing things out of proportion. One way kids can distract themselves is through 'wishing away' the bad thoughts.

5.   Don't let one thing spoil everything

Help your child to park his or her bad thoughts somewhere when they are worried or fretting over something unpleasant. The ability to compartmentalise bad events and keep them from affecting other areas of our life is a powerful coping skill. Resilient sports-people such as golfer Greg Norman and former cricketer Shane Warne have the ability to segment their lives and prevent personal issues from impacting on their sporting performance.

Kids can be encouraged to do the same. For instance, if something negative happens at recess at school, your child needs to make sure it doesn't spoil their whole day. They should think about something else when they are in class and revisit their issue later on. Sometimes it helps to write down your worries and go back to them some time later for a new perspective.

My mum had two fantastic sayings that she used to remind me of. She would often say, 'Park your problems for a while and come back to them later on.' I remember that I would feel relieved when she said this, as it gave me permission not to worry. She'd also often say when something unpleasant happened, 'Don't let this wreck your day. It's not that bad.'

I know – it's easy for you to say!

6. Know when to go with the flow

It takes some wisdom to know what you can change and what you can't change about a situation. If you're stuck in traffic knowing you'll be late for an important event, you probably begin to get upset. But hopefully at some point you realise there is nothing you can do. You are going to be late, so you might as well sit back, turn up the radio and let the traffic take its course; go with the flow. Ah, the relief that comes with letting go!

Help kids differentiate between what's worth worrying about and what's not. It's only worth worrying about what's within your control. If something is out of your control, like a traffic jam, there is no point in becoming stressed as it won't get you there any faster.

I've spent a lot of time helping a friend's daughter differentiate between what's worth worrying about and what's not. She is a natural worrier who puts excessive stress on herself, particularly when it comes to examinations, sports and meeting new people.

To help her, I try to focus her concern on things she can control, such as studying before an exam, preparing for a game of sport, or making sure she feels her best before attending new social situations. By taking positive action she has been able to stop worrying about the results of these activities.

215

The notion of letting go of worries, or going with the flow, can have a powerful impact on kids' well-being, changing their physical as well as mental states.

7. Encourage your children to laugh

Humour is a great coping strategy when things don't go according to plan. Encourage your kids to stand back and find a funny side to a tricky situation they may be in. I'm not suggesting that we trivialise situations; rather, we need to develop the ability to find some humour and hope in adversity. Humour is a powerful tool for resilience as it heightens feeling of control. It helps kids reframe a situation and gain some perspective.

Some children take themselves too seriously. Everything they do needs to have a purpose or some meaning. These kids can be hard to live with. They put a great deal of pressure on themselves to perform well all the time. An injection of humour can help them to relax and loosen up. A trip to the movies, a visit to some light-hearted, easygoing relatives or friends, or spending time with an off-the-wall friend who makes them laugh can be the best mental-health tonic you can provide.

8. Helping kids manage their anger

Anger is the one of biggest emotional issues that children face. Children who can learn to manage their anger have a head start on handling fears and other emotions.

Currently, our community is undecided about how to handle anger. In fact, anger is discouraged as we see no place for it in homes, schools or community. 'Civilised people don't get angry' seems to be the accepted wisdom, so we tend to encourage children to bottle up their anger rather than let it out.

Anger needs to be managed rather than simply avoided, because bottled-up emotions don't always dissipate. They simmer away, and may eventually spill over into physical violence or hurtful verbal abuse that backfires on the angry person.

Kids need to learn that anger can be expressed in ways that are not hurtful to anyone, including themselves. Here are six steps that parents can use to help kids of all ages keep their emotions in check and respond safely when they run high:

Understand it. Help kids understand the events and situations that are likely to trigger angry responses. These situations will vary, but may include physical play, not getting their own way and being teased by others. When kids are calm, help them reflect on what triggered a wobbly, so they can take preventative measures next time. This type of self-knowledge is really helpful for older primary-school children and teenagers.

Name it. Help them recognise the physical signs of anger, such as clenched fists and teeth, tension around their shoulders and heavy breathing. Then assist them to develop a vocabulary around anger. 'Mad as a snake', 'About to lose it' and 'throwing a tanty' are some possibilities. Children can probably generate more! Naming emotions promotes good emotional literacy in kids.

Defuse it. Think of how you can defuse anger in kids. Distraction and time-out can be effective for toddlers with short fuses and even shorter attention spans. For older children parents should use diplomacy rather than discipline, when children are obviously angry. You may need to give some kids space before attempting to talk. Listening to their story, validating their right to be mad and focusing on feelings are some ways to defuse anger. Sometimes knowing that someone else understands how you feel is enough to make your anger dissipate.

Choose it. Help children understand that they do have a choice about how they respond to their anger. They may feel like lashing out, but they don't have to get physically or verbally aggressive. Let kids know in clear terms that slamming doors, throwing things and refusing to cooperate are immature ways of displaying anger. Help them to understand that you are on their side, but that they need to choose socially acceptable ways of handling anger.

Say it. Encourage children to express how they feel verbally, rather than bottle things up or become aggressive. The use of 'I' statements is one way of letting others know how they feel. 'I feel really mad when you say nasty things to me. I absolutely hate it!' is one way of being heard and letting the anger out without becoming too verbally unpleasant.

Let it out safely. Boys, in particular, need innocuous physical outlets for pent-up anger. They may go for a run, belt a pillow or play a physical game to let out their frustration. Some kids may even pour their anger into a

letter, some work or a productive activity. Help children
find legitimate outlets.

Parents need to model healthy anger management so children see
firsthand how to behave when they lose their temper. That means
as parents you should take time to listen to each other, talk through
things and find healthy physical ways to let off steam when you feel
yourself getting to boiling point.

The maxim for families who want to learn to manage anger in
healthy ways should be: 'There is nothing so bad that we can't talk
about it. However, there are things we don't do when we are angry.'

9. Make sure they get enough sleep

Many kids today are sleep-deprived. Teenagers, in particular,
don't get enough sleep. Their sleep–wake cycle is delayed by up
to two hours. That is, they are sleepy later and awake later than
when they were children. Most teens secrete melatonin around
11 pm, so they're rarely sleepy much before then. Children
secrete melatonin far earlier than this. Cortisol, the chemical
that wakes them up, is secreted at 8.15 am for many teens. It
seems the teen brain wants to be asleep just when most have
woken up. One US study found that 20 per cent of teens were
asleep in class in the morning, which had catastrophic effects
on their learning. Some US high schools have delayed the start
of school time to accommodate the teen sleep–wake cycle. The
results were startling and immediate, including better learning
outcomes, better behaviour, fewer fights in school and fewer kids
dropping out of school.

It seems that sleep is one thing we can all become educated

about. We take it for granted and often view poor sleepers through a behavioural lens. Better knowledge of the biology of sleep and of sleep patterns, as well as instigating good sleep habits, will go a long way to helping kids and teens get a good night's sleep:

Keep regular bedtimes. Kids may fight this, but be regular and let them stay up a little later on weekends.

Have a wind-down time of up to 45 minutes prior to bed. This includes removing TV and other stimuli, calming down children and limiting food intake (and caffeine for teens).

Have a bedtime routine such as a bath, a story and teeth-cleaning that signal psychologically it is time for sleep.

Keep **bedrooms for sleep** and not for TV. Bedrooms that resemble caves seem to be recommended.

Maximise the **three sleep cues** of darkness (cave-like bedroom), lowering body temperature (baths can be good for this) and melatonin (work within their cycle).

10. The value of self-initiated play

The importance of free play for children is often underestimated. Outside games develop balance, coordination and fitness. Singing and rhyming games promote language development. Board games and puzzles help intellectual development.

Free play at home is therapeutic for children. Play is an important way to express their feelings. When children are young, dress-up boxes, art boxes and other objects and spaces encourage them to use their imaginations and initiative when they play. Older children still enjoy these things, but they often also like board games, outdoor games and sports that challenge them and maintain their interest.

Left to their own devices, children generally attend to about the right ratio of work, rest and play – that is, play before work and just after rest. However, parents may need to be proactive in encouraging certain types of play, and insist that televisions, computers and electronic games be turned off to direct children to more active, creative or interactive pursuits.

Children generally enjoy playing with their parents. The key for parents is to be led by their children, never to turn the play into a lesson, and to allow their kids time to play on their terms.

To help make sure children enjoy some free play:

Place a **limit** on the number of extra-curricular activities that children are involved in. When a child wishes to exceed the limit, it may be reasonable to ask what they wish to omit from their current schedule.

Resist buying children too many complicated gadgets and electronic toys. Children need **simple objects**, toys, books, rhymes and puzzles so they can interact with and manipulate them.

Have a **technology-free day** once a week. This is the day that the only technology used in the house is for cooking, transport or communication. Games and entertainment must be found in simpler pursuits.

Play with children yourself for enjoyment. Be patient if your child wants to repeat the same game or activity over and over.

Chapter 9

Help them bounce back from hardships and difficulties

Introduction

Kids typically face hardships, frustrations and difficulties (the HFDs I talked about earlier) as they go through different developmental stages. These include changes in routines, social disappointments and loss of friendships. How stressful these everyday events are for children will depend on their coping skills, and their home and school environments.

Major HFDs happen from time to time, such as divorce, illness or moving home. At these times, children and young people need extra support to develop resilient attitudes and skills. This doesn't mean adults should mollycoddle them. However, it does mean that they need more of our energy and focus for a time.

Here are five ways to support kids who are experiencing significant hardships in their lives:

1. **Be attentive.** Listen to them and try to get them to talk. Some kids will refuse. Respect that, but look for ways to get around it. At times of significant hardship, kids need at least one adult who will hang in there with them and help them process events.

2. **Normalise things as quickly as possible.** Sometimes children personalise events, believing that they caused them. As we've seen, pessimists typically attribute bad events to themselves ('It's my fault I have no friends') rather than to circumstances ('They are an unfriendly lot in that football club'). Some kids also catastroph-ise ('This is the worst thing ever') and over-generalise events ('Everyone is against me'). Make them thinking

rationally by checking their facts and letting them know that others have gone through the same situations and survived. This aspect of keeping hope alive is important.

3. **Keep up their confidence and help them get on with life.** The really hard part is getting kids back on the metaphorical horse once they have fallen off. Don't allow them to feel sorry for themselves, or accept extreme negativity, but keep their confidence up and let them know that this hardship will pass. It always does.

4. **Pump up the positives.** How do you cope when life throws you curveballs? Let your kids know your own coping strategies. Teach your kids social skills, in particular, such as how to seek out friends, how to stand up for yourself and how to be a good friend to others.

5. **Catch them being resilient.** Look for signs of recovery, perseverance, disclosure (talking about the bad stuff), handling disappointments and checking facts rather than jumping to conclusions. These are resilient behaviours, which can be pointed out to kids.

Resilience is about coping now and building strengths for the future. There is no doubt that the skills kids learn when they experience small HFDs stand them in good stead when the bigger stuff comes their way.

Seeing life as a series of learning experiences is part of the mindset when you parent for resilience.

1. Coping with change

Life is full of changes. Some are welcome and some aren't. It's human nature to resist change, particularly when it's not welcome. But change presents opportunities to grow and develop. Kids are generally very adaptable, but some changes they experience can be unsettling and confusing.

Children and young people typically experience change they expect and change that comes out of the blue. Expected change involves events such as joining a club, progressing from one class to another, a move that's been anticipated for some time. These changes, while disruptive, aren't generally too stressful for kids. In fact, they offer children opportunities to grow and develop. For instance, changing classes exposes kids to new teachers, different routines and requires them to be flexible and adaptable. Most kids cope with these changes when they are supported by attentive, positive adults.

Unexpected or more dramatic change is more difficult and can be traumatic for kids. A sudden move interstate, or a family death or breakdown is likely to significantly impact on your child.

Kids go through four phases when they experience dramatic or unwelcome change. The first phase is **denial**, when they may refuse to think about the change, or even want to talk about their new school or their parents divorcing. This is quite normal, so it's best to let this phase take its course, while giving your kids lots of factual information. Explain what to expect and suggest tasks they can take on to adjust to the change. Make time to discuss the change rather than just dropping it into conversation and give them time to let things sink in. Listen carefully to what your child has to say; acknowledge his feelings.

The second phase is **resistance**, which can be disturbing for parents. Kids can be angry, depressed or anxious during this phase. They may even blame you for causing the unwanted change, and not caring about their feelings. Reassurance that things will get better and a 'thick skin' are your best allies at this point. Children need time to assess their loss before they can cooperate and work towards adjusting. If you want your child to open up to you, share your own experiences of how you feel or have felt in the same circumstances: 'I felt nervous when I had to start my secondary school, is that how you are feeling now?'

The third phase involves **exploration**. Kids accept that they are changing schools or that their parents are splitting up, so they begin to make plans for the new circumstances. Now you can invite input from your child as to how he or she would like the new circumstances to be. For example, how they will get to school, and what type of uniform they will need. Kids will waver between confusion and enthusiasm during this phase, so you need to keep them busy preparing.

The fourth phase is **commitment**. This is where kids accept the new circumstances and commit to making things work. At this stage you should help them set some long-term goals that will help them settle into their new surroundings or circumstances. Perhaps a child going to a new school can consider the clubs or groups he may join when he's settled in.

When children undergo significant change, it helps to keep some things in their environment unaltered, so they have something familiar to retreat to or to look forward to. If there is disruption in many areas of their life, try to keep some small but fundamental things normal, such as a regular mealtimes and bedtimes, so that they feel anchored to some familiar routine. This is particularly important when kids have experienced loss.

2. Dealing with loss

Kids may experience many different kinds of loss, including a friend who moves away, the death of a beloved pet, or of a loved one. Although death is the most permanent loss we face, there are other forms of loss that can be devastating as well. The most common for children are suddenly moving house or school, and the divorce of their parents. Helping kids deal with loss is something that all parents experience from time to time. While nothing really prepares kids for the loss of a loved one, helping them cope with the smaller losses, such as the death of a pet, does help when a more significant bereavement occurs.

Loss by its very nature involves pain. An anticipated death, separation or move is a little easier for kids to cope with, as they have time to think, mourn and anticipate how they will react. When loss is sudden, there is more confusion and distress because there is much less time for them to adjust. The pain from a loss is also related to the nature of the relationship. A child experiences the most distress when he is close to and dependent on the one he is separated from. If a move or separation takes away the child from the loved one, he may experience the same intensity of pain as if a death had occurred.

Loss involves a grieving process, which is our natural reaction to something that reshapes our world. Grief impacts on our emotions, our behaviour and our thinking. For kids, grief has two requirements. First, they need to process the event that led to loss: 'Will Daddy ever come back?' 'Could I die too?' Second, they need to mourn the loss: 'I wish Grandma was here to read me a story.' Children frequently experience fear and sadness after loss. They fear the future and the unknown and they feel sad for the loss of a loved one, or the more preferable past.

Often adults are grieving the same loss, so assisting kids through such difficult circumstances is tremendously challenging. Here are some general guidelines when children experience a significant loss, such as the death of someone close to them:

Talk about the death or loss. Share important facts about the event. Attempt to get a sense of how your kids feel about the situation.

Share some of your own feelings and thoughts. Sometimes children act as if they have not heard anything you have said when experiencing loss, but they probably have. Nonetheless, be prepared to repeat the same information again and again, as kids often don't process information when they are distressed, or they need to keep hearing your words of reassurance.

Invite children to talk about the feelings they have regarding the event or death. Then you can let them take the lead as to when, how long, and how much is to be discussed.

Reassure them that feelings of sadness and helplessness are normal. A basic understanding of the grieving process can be reassuring to kids, and can provide hope that they will not always feel the way they do.

Involve them in the rituals, including the funeral.
There are no hard and fast rules here, but involvement
can help them move through the grieving process. Most
children, even preschool-aged children, can handle going
to a funeral (although they should never be forced to
go). If something like a funeral seems too overwhelm-
ing for your child, or if he doesn't want to go, you can
create your own ritual or memorial service later. If you
do intend to take your child to the funeral, be sure to
prepare him in advance for what is going to happen
and be ready to answer any questions that he may have
during the service.

Dealing with loss is a long journey and children usually go through
the same stages of grieving as adults, but it's not always a continual process. Kids may be sad one minute but later appear happy
and carefree. Some kids act out, develop behavioural problems or
withdraw after the death of a loved one. At times like these, it is
best to be empathetic and let your son or daughter know that you
feel sad too. You can also explain to them that your sadness sometimes makes you get angry or lose your patience.

If behaviours and emotions are still extreme after six months,
it's probably time to see a professional to help you and your child
cope with the loss.

3. Failure is good for kids

Failure is part of learning, yet it's something most parents and kids
like to avoid. No one deliberately sets out to fail, but any field of
endeavour can take frequent attempts to master.

Some kids are blessed. Whatever they tackle, they seem to succeed at. Others are not quite so lucky. School, sport and social activities can be a struggle for some kids. They just don't get things right the first time. As frustrating and, at times, heart-breaking as it is for parents to watch a child struggle to attain even mediocre levels of success at school, in their sport or leisure activities it's worth remembering that, as we've seen, persistence pays. Here are some ideas to keep in mind if you are parenting a child where success at school, sport and other common childhood activities doesn't come naturally:

Be your child's cheerleader. Kids who have to work really hard to achieve need someone in their lives who can boost their self-confidence. Make a fuss over small successes so they can puff up their chests every now and then.

Focus your comments on contribution, improvement and effort. It's difficult to praise kids when the results aren't there, but you can always focus your comments on their contribution or the effort they make.

Remember that persistence pays. Children who persist learn an important life lesson – that is, success in most endeavours takes effort. Those kids who sail through their childhoods without raising a sweat can struggle when eventually they do have to work long and hard to succeed.

Don't put kids on pedestals. It is difficult living in the shadow of a superstar, so avoid making a huge fuss over the achievements of a particular child – it makes life difficult for those who follow. Recognise results, but balance that by focusing equally on their efforts.

Raising kids who find life a breeze is easy. However, parenting kids who take longer to mature, or kids who must put in 110 per cent effort to achieve, is challenging for any parent.

4. Handling rejection and disappointment

One of the keys to functioning socially and emotionally is the ability to deal with disappointment and rejection.

Most children experience some type of rejection from their peers during their childhood. One study found that even popular children were rejected about a quarter of the time when they made friendly overtures to children at their school.

Most children recover from such rejection. They move on and form constructive, worthwhile relationships. But some kids need help. They take rejection personally, blaming themselves. As a parent, it is useful to challenge this kind of unhelpful thinking and emphasise to your child that they should not be discouraged by casual rejections. Parents can help children understand that rejection may happen for any number of reasons, which are unrelated to them.

In the course of a school day, children will meet challenges and setbacks. They may struggle with some schoolwork. They may not do well in a test or be excluded from a game they wanted to play. Children grow stronger when they overcome such setbacks. The challenge for parents is to build and maintain their child's confidence to help them get through the rough times.

Talk through problems or difficulties, recognising and accepting your kids' feelings. Discuss various scenarios and possible outcomes. The age of your child will determine the amount of detail you go into. Keep things simple and avoid burdening a younger child with concepts he or she doesn't understand.

Your attitude can make a huge difference to how your child reacts to setbacks. If you see rejection or disappointments as problems, he or she will be hamstrung by this view. See them as challenges or try to make light of them, then your child will, in all likelihood, pick up your upbeat view. After all, confidence is catching!

Try the following four strategies:

Model optimism. Watch how you present the world to children, as they will pick up your view.

Tell children how you handle disappointment and rejection. It is reassuring for them to know that you understand how they feel. They can learn a great deal by how you handle situations.

Remind children of occasions in the past when they bounced back from disappointment. Help them recognise those same strategies can be used again.

Laugh together. Humour is a great coping mechanism. It helps to put disappointment in perspective and to understand that things will get better. They always do.

Kids who take the rejection personally can benefit from learning better ways to handle conflict. Let's take a look . . .

5. Dealing with conflict

Helping kids deal with conflict effectively and peacefully is a challenge for many parents. Children's disagreements at home and at school can be noisy, physical and psychologically hurtful. The approach to conflict resolution that we learn and practise in childhood often stays with us for life. Conflict is part of daily living. Effective people resolve conflict in ways that preserve relationships, honour feelings and lead to a satisfactory resolution. They neither avoid conflict nor do they use power to dominate others or win.

When two children have a disagreement that is upsetting to one or both of them, they may need adult assistance to resolve the conflict. There are three things parents should focus on when their children fight:

> **Focus on emotions.** 'You seem upset that your brother . . .' There is nothing better than being understood, so allow your kids to get things off their chests about their siblings. As we saw earlier, effective families work on the principle that there is 'nothing so bad we can't talk about it, but there are behaviours we don't indulge in'. So we can talk about how disappointed or sad you may feel about your sister reading your private diary, but you can't hit or punch her because she did so.

> **Fix the problem.** Help kids to fix their problem or disagreement rather than become involved in it. This is a subtle but potent difference. Stay problem-focused rather than person-focused.

Restore relationships. Restoration should be your focus as a parent after fights. This doesn't necessarily mean your kids must apologise – it's more about how they get on with each other in the future.

Now, here is a five-step conflict-resolution process you can follow to help kids to resolve conflict. It's based on two basic principles. First, those who own the problem solve the problem, with some parental help. Second, child-set solutions are always more effective than those set by adults because kids are more likely to stick to ideas they own in some way:

Control emotions. Emotional containment is a priority. Get kids to calm down before you help them work out the problem. This may mean they sit for a while on their own or go outside and physically let off steam. Once their emotions are contained, you can get down to business.

Communicate thoughts and feelings. Get kids to state the dispute as they see it. Kids generally want to be heard, so listen to their side of the story and, again, try focusing on how they feel about it. Give their emotions a name or label. 'It sounds like you're pretty angry about it. Would I be right?' Once they've acknowledged why they were cross, it's much easier to resolve the issue: 'Okay, you can play with your sister's old toys, but she doesn't want you playing with her new toys for a while. They're special.'

Encourage kids to see the other side of the story.
This step is an important part of any conflict resolution process and encourages a level of empathy: 'Why
do you think your sister may have done that?' 'What do
you think your brother wants?'

Search for a solution. Brainstorm possible suggestions
or ideas both parties can live with. This takes goodwill
and willingness to give ground.

Agree to . . . something. This is the hard one. Ideally,
it's best for kids to come up with their own solution. If
not, don't be afraid to dole one out for them, based on
all that you have heard.

Teaching children some simple rules for resolving conflict may well
be one of the best investments in time and energy that a parent can
make.

6. Handling bullying

Bullying is a word that's wrapped in emotion.

It's been estimated that around 40 per cent of people have
experienced some type of bullying in the past, so for them the word
is inevitably associated with unpleasant memories.

The ghosts from the past are never far away for parents
and can often influence the way we react to difficulties our own
children might experience with others inside or outside school.

Bullying is insidious behaviour that violates our children's
natural right to feel safe and secure. It can adversely affect their
learning, emotional well-being, peer relationships and their sense

of self. It takes many forms and guises, including physical and emotional abuse, intimidation, harassment and exclusion. And it now has a well-publicised cyber dimension, which has moved the goalposts for many kids. In the past, children could escape bullying by staying at home. Cyber-bullying now means this is no longer the case.

Bullying is not the domain of one gender. Girls bully just as much as boys, but they do it in less physical ways. While boys are likely to use physical intimidation or verbal abuse to wield power, girls are more likely to use exclusion or verbal sarcasm to assert themselves.

Bullying should not be confused with teasing, rejection, random acts of violence or physicality and conflict. While children will often tease or fight, this is not bullying. Bullying is about lack of power, as one person is powerless to stop the verbal or physical abuse. It is the selective, uninvited, repetitive oppression of one person by another person or group. It should not be tolerated, or ever practised, by adults or other children.

If you think your child is being bullied, handle the situation with care as some children don't want to admit this is happening to them. It helps to be on the lookout for warning signs, such as items being stolen, your child requesting that the route they take to school is changed, or withdrawing from their usual activities.

If your child is being bullied:

Listen to their story. Take them seriously and avoid dismissing their complaints. Use common sense to differentiate between bullying and more random, non-selective antisocial acts. Kids can be nasty to each other, but nastiness doesn't constitute bullying.

Deal with their feelings. A child who is bullied probably feels scared, angry and sad. Boys are more likely to display anger and girls sadness. The intensity of their emotion is an indicator of how much they are being bullied. Recognise and validate their emotions. Let them talk about what they think (boys respond better to 'think' language) and how they feel. It's normal to feel sad, scared or just plain confused.

Get the facts. Get a clear picture of who is involved, the frequency and what happens prior to and during any bullying. Get your child to be as specific as possible by asking good questions. An accurate picture will help you determine your next course of action.

Give them coping skills. With a clear picture, you can start giving your child some help with how he or she may deal with the bullying, including ways to avoid it, being more assertive and changing poor body language.

Get the school involved. Bullying is best handled when parents and teachers are involved. Some parents tell me that schools can be reluctant to become involved, but from my experience, schools take bullying very seriously and go to great lengths to support and empower those on the receiving ends. Also, they should and usually will look for ways to change the behaviour of bullies. Approach your school through the appropriate channels, make yourself aware of their anti-bullying procedures and programs, and be willing to work within these guidelines.

Help build your child's support networks. Kids need a group of loyal friends to support them when they experience bullying, so look for practical ways to broaden their social groups.

Build their self-confidence. Provide children with systematic encouragement. Reassure them that they will get through this period.

It's worth remembering that children who experience some form of bullying often come out stronger, more empathetic and more resourceful because they have experienced these difficulties and they know they can defeat them.

In conclusion

Currently, parents are under fire from many quarters for the way they are raising their kids. 'Child-centric parenting', 'Afraid to upset kids', 'Outsourcing parenting', 'Parents without backbone', 'Overprotective', 'Too willing to indulge their every whim'. The list of uncomplimentary remarks is a long one!

I don't wish to add to this list, but I must admit that for some time I've been concerned about how modern kids are raised. In two decades as a full-time parenting educator I've seen a seismic shift in parenting styles. We moved away from a style where kids were expected to fit in to their parents to one where it seems imperative that parents not only fit in with their children, but want to please them as well.

The main parenting issues I faced two decades ago revolved around under-parenting, where kids were left to their own resources as parents became increasingly disengaged from them. Now, over-parenting is perhaps the biggest issue, where many parents are too involved and have too large a stake in their children's lives. It's quite a big shift in a short time.

I wrote at the start of this book that there's currently a lot of confusion among well-meaning parents about the best way to raise kids. 'Should I be soft or firm?' 'How do I set boundaries?' 'How do I get my child off to a good start?' This confusion and uncertainty leads to a lack of confidence, which impacts on children.

Parents don't so much lack parenting skills nowadays; it's more that they lack an understanding of their place in the adult–child relationship. 'How can I be my child's friend as well as his parent?' is a modern dilemma. The answer is quite simply, you can't. Well, not always. Being a parent means you won't always please your kids. Sometimes you do upset them, and they really do hate you, even if momentarily. 'You may not like my decision, but you must accept it' is an idea that children of all ages need to become more accustomed to.

Parental anxiety has replaced guilt as the predominant negative parenting emotion. Parents are anxious to get their parenting right so their kids get the best possible start in life. There's anxiety around child safety, as well as anxiety around children being harmed emotionally for life if they are exposed to unpleasant events, actions or words. The propensity to protect children is doing more harm than good. Children are tougher than most of us give them credit for. They are resilient by nature (some more resilient than others). This natural resilience is inhibited by parental over-indulgence, over-involvement and over-investment in their children's well-being.

This book presents a way forward for parents; a set of principles and sensible strategies to help you to raise well-adjusted kids, who are capable of handling some of the difficulties that life dishes up, and who will make a decent contribution to their community, of which they will be a part. The ideas I've put forward move you away from the current child-centric, narrow approach, to a more family-centric approach to raising kids.

Kids need strong leadership, and first and foremost that should come from parents. They need parents who use an authoritative, sometimes tough, approach, where nurture is mixed with firmness and the word 'No' is heard routinely in their homes. They need parents who understand that redundancy is their aim and who employ big-family principles to raise their kids.

Jessica and George are two parents who use the thriving principles I've written about. Their three primary-school-aged children are at times difficult but more often delightful. Independence is a core family value and very much part of their family culture. Both parents spend a lot of time assisting their kids to develop the self-help skills needed for independence. Getting themselves up each morning, preparing snacks, making their own breakfast, packing school bags and putting dirty clothes in the laundry were the types of tasks expected of each child from an early age. They resist the urge to rescue them if they fail to, for instance, remember their lunch money. Instead, they either let their kids experience the consequences of their choices or speak with them to assess whether their expectations are reasonable. Then they make adjustments if they are needed.

Jessica and George have worked hard to develop a strong family orientation towards compromise and considering the rights of others, rather than allowing their children to grow up with an exaggerated sense of entitlement. They developed this sense using the triangle of parenting success outlined at the start of the book. For instance, when eleven-year-old Jenna, the family's eldest, began to take over the family computer, her mother asked her to consider how this impacted on her family.

This family chose a range of family management and behavioural techniques that support the family-first principle over a more child-centric approach. These include an identifiable set of family rituals, such as sharing at least five meals a week and holding regular family meetings. The children are expected to help at home on a regular basis without being paid, and are encouraged to resolve arguments and repair relationship breakdowns with their siblings when they occur. 'What will you do now to fix things up with your brother or sister?' is a response that their children hear often following a sibling dispute.

Effective parenting is easier to write about than to put into practice. I've raised three kids of my own and I know how hard it is to stick to a plan or come up with an appropriate response when your kids won't cooperate at seven o'clock in the morning, or they challenge you verbally late at night when you're dog-tired. It's also hard to stick to a plan when you are stressed, which parents invariably are at times. It helps then to trust your instincts and be intuitive with your parenting.

The thriving way of parenting I've presented is an intuitive, common-sense approach that encourages you to take your place as a wise yet firm leader; to use a managerial style that takes note of your children's opinions, but also allows you to trust your gut instinct and make decisions in the best interests of your child. I've been talking and writing about this approach for some years now and people feel a sense of relief when they hear about it. I get feedback such as: 'It's common sense.' 'You mean it's okay to be the bad guy.' 'It's great not to have to take on all my kids' problems as my own.' Such comments indicate relief as we take back some of our parenting power, and stop being constrained by a type of parental political correctness that stifles our instincts.

It's worth reiterating that parenting is a marathon, not a sprint. It takes time to raise a well-adjusted child. Kids change as they grow and mature, some quite dramatically. Some children can be quite challenging for parents behaviourally and even confidence-wise when they are young, yet they can grow into beautifully behaved, well-adjusted adults. Conversely, easy-to-raise children can become tearaway teenagers for a time before settling down into mature adulthood. The growth of a child is accompanied by a parent's growth: each new situation you encounter is a learning experience for you. That's why the modern imperative to get parenting right immediately is unrealistic. So build some down time into your life. Create some opportunities to reflect on your parenting practice, aim for small improvements and don't be too hard on yourself when you don't get everything just right.

Take your rightful place as parent of your children, develop the behaviour and attitudes to be successful, and learn to cope with the hardships and hurdles that kids throw your way – that's what parenting to thrive is about!

References

P. 4

Australian Bureau of Statistics, *Australian Demographic Statistics 2006 Census*, ABS

P. 92

Australian Temperament Project 1983–2000, Margot Prior, Ann Sanson, Diana Smart, Frank Oberklaid, Australian Institute of Family Studies

P. 102

Centre for Economic Performance discussion paper 311, D. Robertson and J. Symons, 1996

P. 116

'Corporate Paedophilia: sexualising children by advertising and marketing', Clive Hamilton, Australia Institute, 2006

P. 121

Children: The Challenge, Rudolf Dreikurs, Hawthorn Books, New York, 1964. Dreikurs spoke and wrote often about 'the courage to be imperfect'. There are many references to it in this landmark book.

P. 146
Australian psychologist Professor Paula Barrett claims that one in every five children are born with a sensitive temperament. Barrett is the creator of a very successful program that treats anxiety in children. I read this in *Education Today*, Australia, October 2007.

P. 219
A recent study at Drexel University of students aged between twelve and eighteen found that 'twenty per cent of those studied got the recommended eight or more hours of sleep during school nights, with the rest getting less than eight hours. The average sleep for US adolescents is seven hours.' A study of Rhode Island teenagers found that 'eighty-five per cent were chronically sleep-deprived and accumulated a minimum ten-hour sleep deficit during the week. Forty per cent went to bed after 11 pm; twenty-six per cent said they usually got less than 6.5 hours on school nights.' Thus, sleep deprivation in teens is causing growing concern among researchers, educators and parents.

More information

I hope you enjoyed this book and that it got you thinking about parenting in the thriving way. But there's plenty more to learn.

To find out more about thriving parenting (and the associated tough-love approach) and how you can put it into practice, visit www.parentingideas.com.au

One way of staying in touch is to subscribe to my newsletter, Happy Kids, available on my website. For some edgier stuff, read my blog at www.parentingideas.com.au/blog

One Step Ahead

978 174051 026 4

Good parenting isn't instinctive. It's something you learn by trial and error.

But a little guidance on what to expect from young children goes a long way to helping you be confident and effective. Michael Grose identifies the behavioural and developmental issues that most often cause concern and shows you how to work through them by:

- Understanding your child's behaviour and individuality
- Teaching your child social and physical skills
- Giving your child the freedom to learn from mistakes
- Encouraging your child's sense of responsibility and self-discipline
- Involving your child in family decision-making and conflict resolution
- Communicating positively and acknowledging achievements
- Establishing routines—and getting your kids to stick to them

Michael, who is a parenting expert and father of three, also provides helpful and practical advice on all sorts of specific problems, from bed-wetting to fussy eaters, from swearing and tantrums to making friends. He outlines the various stages and ages at which these problems are likely to occur and shows you how to keep your cool by staying one step ahead.

ONE STEP AHEAD

Raising 3–12 Year Olds

MICHAEL GROSE

From the author of *Raising Happy Kids*, *Working Parents*,
A Man's Guide to Raising Kids and *Great Ideas for (Tired) Parents*

Why First-borns Rule the World and Last-borns Want to Change It

978 174051 198 8

This ground-breaking book reveals how birth order is also a vital factor in determining our character and the life we lead.

Did you know that first-borns are more achievement-oriented and responsible than those born after them? That middle children are most likely to buck the family trend? That later-borns are more gregarious and easygoing than their older siblings? Or that those born last are often babied, affectionate and uncomplicated?

Are you nodding as you read this – or outraged by such generalisations? This book also provides:

- Marital advice – when two last-borns marry or form a partnership, you can be sure that they will have a good time together . . . for a while

- Sibling management skills – how to manage your older brother's dethronement syndrome

- Parenting advice – why you should never compare a second-born to her sibling

- Fascinating dinner-party conversation – why first-borns are more prone to heart disorders

Why First-borns Rule the World and Last-borns Want to Change It will help you get the jump on your siblings, friends and even enemies.

WHY FIRST
BORNS
RULE THE
WORLD

AND LAST
BORNS
WANT TO
CHANGE IT

MICHAEL GROSE